Rabindranath Tagore
and Japan

Rabindranath Tagore And Japan: Collected Essays

Kyoko Niwa

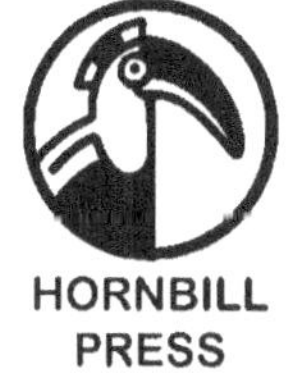

HORNBILL
PRESS

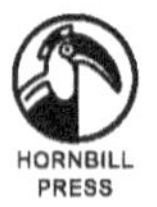

HORNBILL
PRESS

Kolkata, 2022

Japan-India Friendship Series
Editorial Advisor: Nilanjan Bandyopadhyay

Published by Hornbill Press
An imprint of Atmajaa,
Basantakusum, Ariadah, Kolkata-700057
www.atmajaa.com

Cover designed by Studio Kokoro, Santiniketan
Typeset in Garamond and Arunima

ISBN: 978-93-87885-45-5
Price: 650

*To my dear students and friends
in Japan and India*

Rabindranath Tagore has remained my principle interest of research besides teaching of Bengali in Japan, specifically to the Japanese learners nearly over the last three decades. I was rather hesitant in compiling my previously published essays in a book. However, this book is the result of the desire of my friends in India to find my essays on Rabindranath and Japan in a single volume. I am glad that this book is being published on the occasion of the seventieth anniversary of Japan's diplomatic relations with India, as if as a ray of hope in the middle of a deadly pandemic that has shaken the entire world.

Kyoko Niwa
Tokyo University of Foreign Studies
23 February 2022

Rabindranath And Japan

Introduction

It was not long ago that Japan's whole understanding of the world revolved around three countries—India, China and Japan herself. For Japan, China had been perhaps the only civilisation she had known, and considered the country a model nation worth emulating. As for India, it was the land of Buddha beyond China. There had been almost no direct relationship between India and Japan; but the image of India for the Japanese was one of mystery and reverence.

This world view of Japan was overturned completely around the year 1868, during the time of Western influence that began with the initial steps taken by Japan towards modernisation. China and India were dislodged from their earlier position of ideal states and no longer considered to be among countries to be looked up to. Furthermore, colonised India was even seen as a 'ruined nation' with some disrespect, and people firmly determined that their own country should never make the same mistake.

In this context, we can justifiably presume that Japan would have never given the same attention to Rabindranath Tagore without the Nobel Prize, the award that came from the West. Indeed, Tagore was even called a poet from a ruined nation' when he first visited Japan. This distorted perception was one of the reasons why his visits to Japan failed to succeed. Not only did his lectures in Japan not receive due attention, there was confusion and controversy over Tagore and his works.

It is well known that the poet himself had once got involved in a controversy over the China-Japan War with Noguchi Yonejiro. During the war, Tagore was regarded by the authorities as a person belonging to the enemy side, so there was a proclivity to ignore him. However, after the end of the war, this attitude changed and a younger generation of scholars, translators and readers began to take a fresh look at his works.

A hundred years have now passed since the world discovered Rabindranath Tagore. And we can see for a fact that like any other country, in Japan too, the evaluation of Rabindranath has been greatly affected by the course of history. However, there also have been a number of intellectuals, translators and readers who sincerely tried to discover and introduce the true value of Rabindranath, irrespective of the prevalent social condition or context.

Here we are going to trace, chronologically, the social context of Tagore's reception in Japan together with the individual efforts made for introducing his works. Finally, we shall try to present some ideas on the future prospect of Tagore's true evaluation.

Reactions to the nobel prize-winning poet and translations from the first period: 1913–15

Though a number of Japanese intellectuals, such as the art critic Okakura Tenshin (1862–1913) and the painter Yokoyama Taikan, (1868–1958), had visited India at the turn of the nineteenth century and got acquainted with Tagore, his literary works had not been introduced to Japan until he received due appreciation in Europe.[1]

The poet Mashino Saburo (1889–1916) was the first Japanese to translate Tagore's poems early in 1913.[2] It is worth noting that Mashino had translated those poems before Rabindranath Tagore was awarded the Nobel Prize when he first came across the works of Tagore published in the English magazine 'The Nation'. Mashino later mentioned that the poet Miki Rofu had written to him appreciating the outstanding talent of Tagore after he published those poems in Japanese translation.[3] However, this impression of Miki Rofu was addressed to Mashino in his private letter, and we can find no other reaction.

The first report of Tagore winning the Nobel Prize headlined 'Noberu shokin-o kakutaru Indo-jin' (An Indian awarded the Nobel Prize) in the *Chugai Eiji Shinbun* (Chugai English Newspaper) on 1 January 1914 was rather insignificant. Translations of his works that appeared at this first stage did not immediately create much impression.

In early 1914, after the report of the Nobel Prize, the critic Uchigasaki Sakusaburo (1877–1947) translated a few of Tagore's poems.[4] This time again, as Uchigasaki himself said, the literary world of Japan "remained silent and there was no reaction or comment."[5] The writer Yoshida Genjiro (1886– 1956) and the writer and translator Miura Kanzo (1883–1960) also played an active role in translating and introducing Tagore at that very early stage. Except Mashino, the other three were Christians and were closely associated with the periodical *Rikugo Zasshi*, a magazine for young Christians, which devoted a number of pages to Tagore.[6] Yoshida briefly served as editor of the magazine, Uchigasaki had always been an important member of the editorial board and Miura was a regular contributor.

Following the translations by Uchigasaki in 1914, other translators also joined the trend of introducing Rabindranath. Translations from *Gitanjali*, 'The Gardener' and *The Crescent Moon* appeared in some other literary magazines. Mashino also continued translating poems from *Gitanjali*, but the first Tagore book to be published was *Sadhana: The Realisation of Life*, translated by Miura Kanzo in 1915.[7] However, this translation was much criticised, especially on the ground that Miura was not an expert in Indian philosophy as was pointed out by Kimura Taiken (1881-1930), a renowned scholar of Indian philosophy of his time.[8]

Soon after *Sadhana* was translated, Mashino published the complete translation of *Gitanjali*.[9] Miura, who had earlier translated *Sadhana*, also published his own complete *Gitanjali* under a different title.[10] Both these versions were criticised by some scholars, mainly on account of mistranslation. Besides, there was even a heated argument between these two translators. Mashino, on his part, criticised Miura saying he considered Rabindranath as a Buddhist so easily because of not knowing anything about Indian philosophy and the Brahmo Samaj, while Miura, on the other hand, attacked Mashino's translation by saying, "I cannot bear seeing these serious mistakes" without any further specification.[11]

In 1915, the rumour of Tagore's visit to Japan triggered off an explosion in the publication of his works as well as articles focusing on these works. This phenomenon later came to be known as the 'Tagore boom'. The focus shifted beyond *Sadhana*, *Gitanjali*; with *The Crescent Moon*, *The Gardener*, *The Post Office* and *The King of the Dark Chamber* being translated into Japanese one after another in 1915; it culminated in the publication of *The Complete Works of Rabindranath* at the end of the year. This was, however, not a complete collection of Rabindranath's works. Though all these translations were done from English, they became instrumental in gradually introducing the poet to the literary world of Japan.

In Japan, no major writers or poets had taken on the task of translating Tagore's works at that early stage. Moreover, following this early introduction of Rabindranath, the 'Tagore boom' triggered off a heated controversy, not so much on his literature, but on his philosophy—more specifically on the question if his ideas were valuable to the Japanese or not.

When we survey the reviews of the translations or articles on the poet, we can easily notice by looking through the titles that quite a lot of them were written on the philosophical aspects of Tagore. Just before he was introduced to Japan, Henri Bergson and Rudolf Eucken had been welcomed as eminent philosophers by Japanese intellectuals. This was about the time when the enthusiasm for these two had cooled down so that there appeared some articles comparing Rabindranath Tagore with Bergson or Eucken. A renowned critic, Nakazawa Rinsen (1878–1920), was one of those who studied Tagore's philosophy and gave him the epithet, 'Bergson of the East.'[12] Nakazawa also described Tagore as a 'Pantheist'. However, Mashino and other translators showed much dissatisfaction with these statements. Contradicting these observations, some scholars of Indian philosophy expressed their difference of opinion by quoting from the Upanishads. Among them was Kimura Taiken, who tried to explain the background of Tagore's philosophy by referring to his association with the Brahmo Samaj together with the Upanishads and Buddhism in India.

In these circumstances, 'Sadhana' was naturally the book which was the most talked about. Even when they referred to *Gitanjali*, the philosophical aspect of the poetry was the main subject and there was hardly any discussion of the poetic qualities. Furthermore, Tagore's other works were hardly discussed.

Tanaka Odo (1867–1932) and Kato Chocho (1886–1938), both literary critics, showed their distaste for this 'Tagore boom'. However, what they said was only about the mood of Japan which superficially raved over the 'Tagore boom' and did not actually enter into the realm of Rabindranath's thoughts or artistic excellence. There was a rather peculiarly mixed reaction among intellectuals as the critic and philosopher Ebu Oson, has described it:

> Some people so uncritically admire Tagore as the admirers in Europe and India. Some people, however, are discriminating in their appreciation of Tagore. But some others try to reduce his importance with a reactionary indifference.[13]

It also should be mentioned here that these discussions took place mainly among scholars and translators, especially among critics and scholars of Indian philosophy and of English literature. The leading writers and poets showed little interest in them.

In these crosscurrents of popularity and adverse reaction, Mashino was one of those rare intellectuals who maintained a sincere interest in Tagore without joining any of the groups. His translations were not always highly praised and he was rather a minor poet who had hardly any influence in the literary world of Japan. But one could not but admit his sincere approach and devotion to Tagore's works. He translated *Gitanjali*, *The Crescent Moon*, and *The Gardener* one after another and humbly accepted the criticisms so that he even retranslated *Gitanjali*. According to his own testament, he came to be acquainted with Tagore and Indian thought about the time he came to know that he had been infected with tuberculosis. The more serious the disease became, the more he was engrossed in translating Tagore's poetry. He passed away just before Rabindranath visited Japan for the first time in 1916 and with the death of this devoted follower, a curtain came down on the first chapter of introducing Tagore in Japan.

First visit to Japan: 1916

Tagore visited Japan for the first time in 1916. Public figures of Japan and India met directly perhaps for the first time. However, probably unexpected by Tagore, there was already to some degree a strain in the relations between the two countries and also a kind of apprehension that the Japanese people would not listen to Tagore's message unbiasedly, as we can see from this statement of Uchigasaki:

> The visit of the greatest poet born in modern India will be a great stimulus for us to take an interest in Indian thought. There is a tendency among the Japanese in general to ignore India's philosophical ideas because of the country's political subjugation, and thus to dismiss Rabindranath as one who has come from a ruined nation. This is a great loss to us.[14]

In the context of the 'Tagore boom' of the previous year, some critics reacted unfavourably to this sudden popularity. In these circumstances, Kato Chocho used the word 'ruinous' to describe Rabindranath in his article 'Tagoru ryuko ni taisuru fuman' (My dissatisfaction with the Tagore boom) published in *Yomiuri Shinbun* for 15-18 May 1915. Uchigasaki did not mention anyone by name, but it is obvious that he was sufficiently aware of the prevailing mood among his countrymen which was to ignore Tagore as a poet from a 'ruined nation'. It is true that the ordinary Japanese had shown some excitement over his visit; but no excitement or interest can be traced among the intellectuals. Furthermore, there must have been a mood of disrespect as we can surmise from Uchigasaki's statement.

Tagore arrived in Japan on 29 May 1916 amid this ambience of conflicting attitudes. After delivering a speech titled 'India and Japan' in Osaka, he went to Tokyo and delivered his major lecture, 'The Message of India to Japan', at the Tokyo Imperial University on 11 June. This was followed by another lecture, 'The Spirit of Japan,' delivered at Keio University in Tokyo on 3 July.

It seems the news of Tagore's visit reached the Japanese people rather late since only a few articles had appeared before his arrival. It was only after the speech at the Tokyo Imperial University that special issues of three magazines were published consisting mainly of the impressions and reflections about him or about his speeches. These three magazines which published their special editions in July 1916 were *Rikugo Zasshi*, *Shincho*, and *Shinjin*. Among these, *Rikugo Zasshi* collected articles from the widest range of people and did not limit itself to prominent writers or scholars only. In *Shincho*, there were as many as eighteen famous writers and poets of the day who presented their impressions of Tagore. In *Shinjin*, there were articles by nine scholars focusing on the lecture at the Tokyo Imperial University.

Tagore's arrival seemed to have caused a renewed 'Tagore boom' and those who were critical of it the previous year once again made unfavourable comments about its reappearance. Poet, novelist and critic Iwano Homei (1873–1920) was one of those who even had an emotional outburst, saying:

> I think it was only a year ago that you (Rabindranath) suddenly gained popularity. This was only because translators and publishing houses were trying to make money by introducing something new. We intellectuals were not really impressed by your poetry or your philosophy since your ideas were very different from those of ours.'[15]

There were of course some intellectuals who were unhappy with such an attitude, and demonstrated their sympathy for Tagore though it did not lead them to take any further interest in his works or lectures.

Probably the most exhaustive work on this subject of f Tagore's visit to Japan and the reaction it provoked is Stephen Hay's *Asian Ideas of East and West*. In the book, Stephen Hay summarised the 1916 visit as follows:

> The next major thrust toward Asian unity was taken by India's leading s poet, Rabindranath Tagore, who visited Japan in 1916 with the express purpose of propagating the idea of a renascent Eastern civilization. He was welcomed enthusiastically by Japan's educated class not because of his friendship with their own Okakura, but because he had been awarded in 1913 one of Europe's highest accolades, the Nobel Prize for Literature. In three public lectures, India and Japan,' 'The Message of India to Japan' and 'The Spirit of Japan', Tagore presented his view of the Oriental civilization to which he assumed both countries belonged. Each Japanese intellectual reacted to Tagore's message in his own way but when all their comments were published it was clear that most of them disagreed with the Indian poet's concept of a spiritual East standing aloof from, and defiled by, a materialistic West. [16]

Stephen Hay put forward a persuasive analysis with his authentic research. However, there remain some misunderstandings which should not be overlooked. We have already seen the distorted circumstances of 1915 and 1916 from which it can hardly be said: 'He was welcomed enthusiastically by Japan's educated class. It is true there was great excitement among ordinary people, but the educated class' remained more or less indifferent. Since they were already indifferent before hearing anything from Tagore, it is worth taking a closer look at their reactions to find out what they were reacting to. Let us examine one such typical statement by an intellectual who remained indifferent to Rabindranath throughout:

> This might not have been the main point of his speech, but considering his attitude as a whole, I think it was one of condemnation of science. At least his followers, I am afraid, will believe it to be so. If this notion gains in strength then I fear that it may undermine our civilization or weaken our resolve to uphold it ... What Japan is today is because we assimilated western civilization as our own. Western civilization is a creation of science. So if we reject science, we have to go backward in the course of history. It may be all right to reject science in one's personal life, but it will be quite dangerous to do so as a nation ... We are not wearing western civilization like a decoration on the surface. It has gone deep into our psyche and has become the flesh and blood of Japan.[17]

This was written by Inoue Tetsujiro, professor of Tokyo Imperial University. He often wrote articles with the purpose of enlightening his people, and we notice the same spirit here. Therefore, we may consider this not so much a response to Tagore, but an appeal to the Japanese. In the same article, he also said that Tagore was from a 'ruined nation', and was denouncing civilisation. He tried to refute that denunciation by saying, 'Especially we, as the people of a rising nation, should banish such Indian notions as pessimism or the weariness of life. Hence we cannot regard this as a direct response to Tagore's speech, but rather a warning to the ordinary people not to follow his ideas.

It is true, as Stephen Hay says, that most of the intellectuals 'disagreed with the Indian poet's concept of a spiritual East standing aloof from, and defiled by, a materialistic West.' Most Japanese intellectuals did not sympathise with Tagore's notion of East and West and this is partly because of the difference in their political situations, one colonised by the West, another established in her independence. It was in this context that critic and philosopher, Tanaka Odo, wrote:

> When there was no political unity in Japan, no readiness in the Japanese army, when our ancestors were enjoying peace, then suddenly those three or four nations of the West, as if it were a bolt from the blue, visited them and threatened them... Our ancestors were told by those nations that they must choose either death or modern civilization. And they chose modern civilization as the only way to escape death. The death which they feared was not physical death but the death of the spirit. What they feared most was yielding to violence or the loss of their independent existence... There was only one motive in our adoption of western civilization and commencement of modernization. That motive, of course, was to maintain our independence against fears of oppression by foreign countries. [18]

Modern civilisation here meant Western civilisation and, in Tanaka's opinion, there was no choice for Japan other than to accept Western civilisation for its independent existence.

We are going to discuss one more article which expresses disagreement with Tagore's notion of 'East and West. The excerpt below is from a piece written by Ebina Dansho (1856–1937), a Christian priest:

India is an old country and Japan is a comparatively new country ... India has many things to be proud of in her history, but Japan has hardly anything in her past and should rather have something she can be proud of in her present and future ... Considering her natural capacity for imbibing other civilizations, I would say that Japan's brothers are not China and India, but England and France. A classification of civilization cannot be easily made by its location.[19]

This statement draws our attention to how its writer looked upon his own country. This may well represent Japanese thinking more generally. What he is proud of is not ancient Japan which had closer ties with China or India, but modern Japan looking to England and France for inspiration. His image of Japan or the East clearly does not strike a chord with Tagore.

Still, Ebina did not totally disapprove of the poet's ideals, or rather he did have some appreciation for Rabindranath as is evident from the following:

However, when the poet said with indignation that the motto of 'the strong (devouring) the weak' must not be allowed in this East though it plays tyrant in the West, he struck a blow to the eagerness for territorial expansion by the Japanese. Those who are bent on such expansion, ridicule him by calling him 'a poet from a ruined nation'. But we should listen carefully to his words. If it were the time when Japan herself was apprehensive of domination by the West, she would have sympathized with the poet. However, today people are no more afraid of being colonized and moreover they themselves are rather ready to attack and invade other nations economically or politically, (so) there are many who naturally abuse the poet's words as 'ruinous.'[20]

This statement is important not only because Ebina appreciated Tagore's humanism, but also because he admitted the rise of militant nationalism in Japan. His statement deserves greater attention because he offered a possible explanation as to why Tagore's words were rejected. True, both India and Japan had faced a cultural crisis when they met the West, but Japan and India went through it in a different way and each country's notion of the 'East' was not always the same.

True, the idea of the East and the West presented by Tagore, as Stephen Hay has explained, was not acceptable to Japan. However, we have to be more careful with the investigation of Stephen Hay concerning the group of Japanese intellectuals about whom he writes:

> The greatest irony in the reaction of Tagore's idea of Asian spiritual revival by his fellow writers in Japan is that those who praised his message most warmly were men like Noguchi, who had been most deeply influenced by English and American Romantics, while those who condemned it most harshly were writers like Kawahigashi and Iwano, who were most deeply committed to the revival of Japanese traditions.[21]

There seems to be no doubt that Noguchi (Noguchi Yonejiro or Yone, 1875–1947) was a representative of the Westernised intellectual and one of the foremost admirers of Rabindranath. But Noguchi was not as simple an admirer of Rabindranath as is generally believed. He came to know Rabindranath in England soon after his poetry had made a great splash in Europe. However, this does not mean that Noguchi played an important role in introducing Rabindranath to Japan. He did not translate any of his poems before 1916. Instead, he wrote four articles on Rabindranath in 1915, but these were not entirely favourable. Let us take a look at an extract from one of these articles:

> At least I cannot find anything new and surprising in Rabindranath's philosophy ... In the East, at least in Japan, the value of Rabindranath is not as much as that in the West. The Western people that [got] in touch with Eastern thought only recently must have found Rabindranath's ideas new and peculiar. However, we Japanese need to investigate our ancestors' efforts and distinguished works before we read Rabindranath's works.[22]

Here, Noguchi does not value Tagore's idea or philosophy highly and he did not change this opinion until the end as we can find almost the same view in his interview recorded in 1929.[23] This view of Noguchi is quite suggestive, in the sense that this can be one of the reasons why people did not listen to Rabindranath's 'message' seriously. Once he considered Tagore as an 'Asian' poet, he lost his earnest desire to know his philosophy or ideas relegating him as one of those wise men he knew from the past. This article was written in 1915 before Tagore's visit to Japan, but indeed this is one of the typical attitudes of Japanese intellectuals throughout the period of his visits.

We are going to look into the relationship between Noguchi and Rabindranath later again and now we should be back to the point of grouping Japanese intellectuals. In the statement quoted above, Stephen Hay only named Noguchi as an intellectual who praised Rabindranath and emphasised that he was "deeply influenced by English and American Romantics". But actually, it was not at all exceptional for Japanese poets and writers in those days to be influenced by Western literature or thought, and it cannot generally be said that it was the Westernised intellectuals who always praised Rabindranath.

For example, Tanaka Odo, whose statement we have quoted earlier, was a philosophy teacher at Waseda University who learned Pragmatism from John Dewey at Chicago University, and Inoue Tetsujiro, whom we have referred to, was an expert on German philosophy. Inoue spent seven years in Germany in his youth and also contributed to the highly-regarded poetry book *Shintai shishu* (poetry of new style) which was the first attempt to translate renowned Western poetry into Japanese and which became a source of modern poetry-making in Japan. These two figures, Tanaka and Inoue, were certainly influenced very much by Western ideas but had never shown any serious interest in Rabindranath and rather reacted unfavorably to the poet.

Stephen Hay mentioned two other names, Kawahigashi Hekigoto (1873–1937) and Iwano Homei (1873–1920) as those who condemned Tagore most harshly and who "were most deeply committed to the revival of Japanese traditions". Kawahigashi, being a 'waka' poet (specialising in a form of classical Japanese poetry), was sincerely committed to the revival of traditional literature. He did not approve of Tagore's speeches on civilisation describing them as 'too optimistic and unsatisfactory in the sense that they do not reflect the agony of Indian people.' [24] However, in the same article he also admitted that he was impressed by the way Tagore spoke. He was indeed a rare poet who actually listened to Tagore's speech. On the whole, his attitude was sympathetic rather than condemning him most harshly.

We have already seen one of Iwano's statements and there is no doubt he was harsh to Rabindranath, though what he was really irritated about was not the poet himself, but the trend of praising him uncritically. However, he cannot be classified as a traditionalist. Unlike Kawahigashi, Iwano was a modern novelist who started his career as a naturalist writer. Later, he opposed other naturalist authors and adhered to his own ideology but his main concern was not the revival of Japanese tradition.

On the whole, irrespective of the influence of Western ideas or not, most of the intellectuals were reluctant to respond to Tagore's 'message,' and even in case they did respond, most of them reacted unfavourably. However, is there anything common to those who supported him?

It has been mentioned that the Christian group of the journal *Rikugo Zasshi* played an important role in introducing Rabindra and indeed this group of Christians was the most attracted to him, including the Christian priest Ebina Dansho mentioned earlier. Another Christian priest Naruse Jinzo (1858–1919) was also an intellectual who supported Tagore, though he did not really join in the controversy. He studied in the United States and afterwards founded Japan Women's University. It was he who invited Tagore to the summer house of the University in Karuizawa to deliver some lectures which were memorised by the students for a long time.

People drawn to Tagore were minorities among the intellectuals, in the sense that they did not have any firm standing in the Japanese mainstream, being people such as Christians, young students or women. In Japan, Westernised did not mean anything exceptional; as we can see from personalities like Tanaka or Inoue, who were 'Westernised' enough in the eyes of the ordinary Japanese, but still had their place in the mainstream. Although Christians like Ebina or Uchigasaki were highly educated, they were much less influential. On the whole, mainstream Japanese intellectuals rejected Tagore not exactly because of what he said, but rather because of the discursive frame of his reception. Even the supporters of Rabindra such as Ebina, could neither share his ideas on civilisation nor agree with his classification of East and West.

The Japanese in general had been accepting Western culture and science quite positively by then and there was little chance of their sharing the image of the materialistic West. Thus, Tagore's warning against militant imperialism was more or less out of tune with those people. Moreover, considering their country rather closer to the West than to the East, there was little inclination to think about Japan's role in Asia in the same way as the Bengali author had defined it. Still, we should not underestimate the influence of Tagore among the voiceless or less influential group of minorities. They crowded the hall where he delivered his speeches, and they listened to him eagerly. The impression of the poet stayed long and deep in their minds and, because of that, Rabindranath was never completely forgotten even during the dark era of war.

Visits and translations from the second period: 1916–29

The first visit of Tagore in 1916 was a stopover on his way to the United States and he again landed in Japan briefly in February-March 1917 on his way back home. His visits in 1924 and 1929 were of much shorter duration. The destination of his 1924 trip was China. Soon after the news of his trip to China was publicised in Japan, the idea emerged that he should be invited to Japan as well. A reporter of *Asahi Shinbun* was sent to Peking with the invitation and after showing some hesitation Tagore finally accepted the offer.[25] Tagore's last visit in 1929 took place in a situation similar to the first one in 1916. He agreed to break his journey on his way to Canada, though he declined to accept any offer to speak because of ill health. He only agreed to attend social gatherings at some places and give brief talks. However, the situation changed dramatically when he cancelled the programme in the United States because of his humiliation at the immigration office. He took a Japanese steamer to sail directly to Japan and on hearing the news, a group of people quickly organised a reception for the poet. After resting for a few days, Tagore finally delivered his five-part lecture, *The Philosophy of Leisure* which was originally planned for the United States.

Although the enthusiasm generated during his visit in 1916 was missing in the 1920s, his lectures attracted many people. In 1924, it was reported that more than two thousand people, mainly students, came to listen to his lecture at the Tokyo Imperial University. In the same year, he also delivered a special lecture for women and, again, the hall was filled up by about two thousand women who came to listen to him.

The literary world of Japan lost its zeal to publish anything on Tagore after 1916, or even if it did publications were less frequent. However, on the occasion of his second visit in 1924, a number of new translations came out, namely, *Sacrifice*, *Gora* and *The Wreck*.[26] Among these, *Gora*, translated by Sano Jinnosuke who had been at Santiniketan for some years, was an epochmaking work in the sense that the translation was done directly from Bengali. This first translation from Bengali was done, according to the translator, with the help of the English translation, but his translation, together with its notes and explanation about the novel and its author, was fairly accurate. He had the good fortune to be able to ask the author himself about the sentences that he did not understand.[27] The novel received an appreciative though not extensively publicized review, which said in part:

> I cannot help feeling sympathy for the social uneasiness that has been described in detail by Tagore. And I also sincerely wish to examine if that uneasiness has anything in common with the reality of our country either in positive or in negative terms. [28]

Unfortunately, this article did not make the due impact because the voice was that of an unknown intellectual. It should, however, be remembered since it contained a new and insightful appreciation of Rabindranath's novels. In addition to the above-mentioned translations, new versions of works that had earlier been translated also appeared around 1924. These versions were the works of famous writers and poets. For example, the playwright Osanai Kaoru (1881–1938) translated *The Post Office*; and the poet

Shiratori Shogo (1890–1973), translated *The Crescent Moon*.

Nevertheless, no special issue of any periodical was published commemorating Tagore's visit in 1924. *Rikugo Zasshi*, which had taken an active role in introducing Rabindranath in 1916, had ceased publication in 1921, and no other magazine seemed to have stepped into the breach in that respect. On the whole, the enthusiasm in introducing Tagore was on a much smaller scale in 1924 than in 1916, and the response was further reduced in 1929.

Controversy over the China-Japan war and oblivion during World War-II: 1937–45

It has been mentioned that Noguchi, who is commonly believed to be an admirer of Tagore, cannot be uncritically regarded so. He had his own independent poetic development and no definite influence of Tagore can be traced in his writings. Noguchi spent almost eleven years, from 1893 to 1904, in the West, mostly in the United States and in England, and published his English poetry books in both countries. His writings were once highly appreciated by a certain literary group in the West. His interest was not confined to the English Romantics; indeed, he had a wide circle of friends among English poets, including some of the Imagist or modernist poets. Noguchi was always active in introducing the new stream of Western literature to

Japan and also played a crucial role in introducing Japanese culture and literature overseas through his great number of essays published in English magazines or lectures delivered outside Japan. He was almost the only poet who formed a personal friendship with Tagore and showed respect for the poet. However, it seems Tagore's English translations did not attract him as much as original English poetry. Being an expert in Western literature and an intellectual who actually lived in the West, he often criticized an easygoing acceptance of Western ideas in Japan. His emphasis on Japan's own cultural identity was all the more strengthened when he made various statements about Japan in the West. He tilted more and more towards Nationalistic ideas throughout the 1920s and 1930s and finally contradicted in strong words Tagore's statement on the China-Japan war.[29] Rabindranath was certainly shocked by Noguchi's refutation and there were a couple of letters exchanged between them on this subject, though neither was successful in convincing the other.

This was not their personal controversy in any way, since both of them represented their own society. As for Rabindranath, there was no contradiction being a Bengali or Indian, as well as being a poet of the world; but for Noguchi, he could not be Japanese as well as a world citizen at the same time and had to make a choice. His choice was to be Japanese:

> What I am afraid of is to be called a betrayer by my fellow countrymen. My belief, contrary to your belief, is that I want to be a true man before I am a poet.

Therefore, it is important to me that I belong to a sovereign country.[30]

Noguchi's reaction shows the atmosphere in Japan at that time that did not allow him to evaluate Tagore positively.[31]

In this period of history, Tagore was considered to be an enemy, or at least of supporting the enemy, and the mood to dismiss him became the primary focus. The poet and translator Yamamuro Shizuka (1906–2000) offers an insight into the political setting of the era:

> I first published Tagore's poetry in 1943 and it was during the time Japan was at war. The inhumane war of aggression was being carried out. ... I intended to resist that, though I had little influence. That is why I translated the works reflecting such profound love and humanity written by this great Asian poet. Tagore was almost forgotten and ignored by then, since he was considered to be belonging to the enemy side; and despite such an adverse situation, an editor of Kawaide shobo dared to publish the book. However, a very strict censorship was imposed during the wartime, and twelve poems were expunged from the collection at the end.[32]

It should be noted here that at the height of the war people like Yamamuro looked at the poet as a symbol of humanism and it was through his personal effort and the bold attempt taken by a publishing company that a new collection of poems came out. The spirit of Rabindranath did not totally vanish and it was silently handed down to the next generation.

Revaluation and translations: 1946–2011

After the last visit of Tagore in 1929, the impact of the poet gradually withered. Moreover, as Japan had taken the path of militarism, as predicted earlier by Tagore, even his name disappeared from public discourse. This uneasy situation was, however, completely overturned after the end of the war, and in the late 1950s we can see the emergence of a new trend of rediscovering Tagore. Yamamuro, quoted above, published a new edition of his translated poetry and others also joined this new tide of publications. [33]

The most significant resurgence of translating and introducing Tagore after 1916 occurred around 1961, on the occasion of the Tagore centenary celebrations. In 1959, a Memorial Society of Rabindranath Tagore was established for the birth anniversary celebrations. Okura Kunihiko, who had hosted Rabindranath in 1929, was its chairman, and Yamamuro Shizuka, Shimonaka Yasaburo, a representative of a publishing company named Heibonsha, and Nakamura Hajime, a scholar of Indian philosophy, were the founder-members of the society. The society published a book of essays in connection with the celebration of the one hundredth birth anniversary, and a bibliography, of works of and on Tagore, was appended. [34] Essays by scholars like Suzuki Daisetsu, a scholar on Zen Buddhism, Tanaka Otoya, a scholar of Sanskrit literature, Ebihara Tokuo, a scholar of French literature and a specialist on Romain Rolland, and Okakura Koshiro, grandson of Okakura Kakuzo, a scholar of international politics, were included in the book.

Several new translations appeared, and a publisher named Apolonsha had planned to print an eight-volume collection of Rabindranath's works. The collection actually started appearing in 1959 and except for the second volume, which never came out, the rest were published by 1961. Among those new translations, the most important work is definitely the complete translation of 'Gitanjali' by Watanabe Shoko (1907–1977) in the third volume of the Apolonsha edition. Watanabe's new translation, directly from Bengali, was not only epoch-making but is recognised till today as the standard translation of Rabindranath's poetry in Japan. This translation was first published in 1961 by Apolonsha and was later reissued in an Iwanami Shoten paperback series in 1977, which is one of the oldest and most authoritative series on world and Japanese literature.

A striking feature of this book is that Watanabe translated not only all the poems of the original *Gitanjali*, but those of the English *Gitanjali* as well. He presented both translations in a single volume so that readers could compare and recognise clearly the fundamental differences between the two. This presentation opened the eyes of readers regarding the poetic genius of Rabindranath. Watanabe, the translator, himself contrasts the Bengali originals with Tagore's English versions and emphasizes the importance of direct translation from the Bengali in the following words:

> If we pay attention to the style of poetry, we can easily notice that all 157 poems of the original 'Gitanjali' were written in various fixed verse forms and had been meant for singing, whereas all 103 poems of the English *Gitanjali* are prose poems ... We see in this English text that many of the repetitions were omitted, peculiar words or phrases of the Indian context were replaced by English idiomatic phrases or style of saying, and sometimes even extra explanations were added ... On the whole, the English *Gitanjali* was deliberately written for English readers. And this is because even those 53 poems that are included in both the original and the English version create so different in impression ... The poems that were left out cannot be the ones the poet himself felt less confident about. We can rather recognize the peculiarity or the greatness of the poet in these poems themselves.[35]

Watanabe pointed out that the English *Gitanjali* was meant for English readers. He implied that Japanese readers can also esteem those poems which were excluded from the English version and he believed that this kind of appreciation would lead them to a real understanding of Tagore's works.

With this effort of Watanabe, the translation of Tagore's works stepped into a new stage, that is, as direct translations from Bengali. This new generation of translators, who were involved in introducing Rabindranath, all knew Bengali well and were scholars of Indian studies. Three such scholars are widely known—Azuma Kazuo, Morimoto Tatsuo and Watanabe Shoko.

Watanabe Shoko, whose complete translation of *Gitanjali* became a monumental publication, was generally known as an expert on Buddhism. He studied Indian philosophy at Tokyo University and became a professor first at Taisho University, and later at Tokyo University. He had a special talent in learning foreign languages and mastered Bengali as well as Sanskrit, German and other languages.

Azuma Kazuo (1931-2011) also studied Indian philosophy and German literature at Tokyo University and learned Bengali from Watanabe in his youth. He was appointed as professor at Waseda University and later at Tsukuba University. Meanwhile, Azuma became known as an expert on Tagore both within Japan and outside. Azuma often emphasized the importance of translating from the original and he himself made many of the translations from Bengali.

Morimoto Tatsuo (b. 1928) has a different background from the above two translators. He studied theology at Doshisha University and came to know Rabindranath during that period. He says that a missionary once recommended him *Gitanjali* and he was completely absorbed in the book right from the moment he started reading it. That was the time just after World War II and he says he had never heard the name of Tagore before. Morimoto worked on Gandhi as well as Rabindranath and has specialized in modern Indian thought. Later he learned Bengali and published his own translation. Among these, the book of Rabindranath's later poems, *Tagoru shiseino uta* (Poems of Life and Death by Tagore), was welcomed especially by senior readers.

Apart from translations, academic study on Tagore also began after the 1970s. Morimoto translated Tagore's biography by Krishna Kripalani an Azuma published a book on Tagore. And all these works of this generation were later compiled into the twelve-volume set of *Tagoru Chosakushu* ('The Collected Works of Rabindranath Tagore'), which started to be published in 1981.

The chief editor of this new collection was Azuma. This is an authentic introduction to Rabindranath, although there are some works that have not been translated. In the twelve-volume collection, two volumes are devoted to poems. We find names of eleven translators including some leading poets like Tamura Ryuichi (1923–98) and Ooka Makoto (b. 1931). Quite a number of the new translations were from English. Other volumes contain short stories, dramas, essays and letters. One volume is a collection of essays on different topics related to Tagore. This is undoubtedly a great achievement through which readers can approach many different aspects of his works. Several short stories, a selection of dramas, poems, a selection of essays and letters, which were translated directly from Bengali, were introduced in Japan for the first time through this collection.

There was no more nation-wide controversy over Rabindranath in this second tide of re-launching the poet. There was a genuine commitment from those who appreciated him, especially scholars specializing in Indian Studies. This time, translations directly from Bengali predominated, unaffected by evaluations from the West. Rabindranath Tagore could not be called a poet of a 'ruined nation' any more, nor could he be dismissed by the standards of Western or English literature. This approach, though new, has opened up the path to the appreciation of Tagore in the context of Indian literature.

Conclusion: Recent reviews on rabindranath and the future rospect

Almost all important works by Rabindranath have already been translated into Japanese, including those that did not find place in the twelve-volume *Tagoru Chosakushu* and have been translated separately, e.g., *Ghare Baire* by Onishi Masayuki and *Shesher Kabita* by Usuda Masayuki. These translators belong to a still younger generation and their translations were done from the original Bengali.

Apart from translations, it can be said that Tagore studies have not matured yet. Except for the two books by Azuma mentioned earlier, there has been only one volume on Rabindranath published so far, written by the present author. Theses and articles published after

World War II are also few in numbers. The above books and articles are not very much more than introductory studies on Rabindranath's life or literature; and there is much to be done, especially in the field of literary criticism.

On the occasion of Rabindranath's 150th birth anniversary, special events and programmes have been organised, though on a much smaller scale compared to the 100th birth anniversary celebrations. Still, some of the events were successful, with full audiences, which was rather unexpected. Publications were also not as profuse as at the 100th anniversary; not because there is no demand for Rabindranath's books, but because most of his works have already been published and are still in print. One of the significant publications in 2011 was the special issue of a magazine *Shi to Shiso* (Poetry and Idea). Celebrating the sesquicentennial anniversary of the poet, this magazine included nine articles on him together with a few new translations of his poetry. More than half of the articles in the magazine are by Indian writers including Sunil Gangopadhyay. This kind of publication was certainly innovative and instructive, but at the same time it shows that there are not many in Japan who are capable or competent enough to write such articles. However, when we turn our eyes to the questions and answers on the same issue, we can see that many poets actually read Tagore and, in most of the cases, are impressed by his poetry. From these instances, we can expect to discover many more potential readers and further serious studies in the future.

It is true that Tagore Studies in Japan have not yet matured as much as that of, say, the study of Goethe or Baudelaire, though the value of Tagore's works is no less than that of those other poets. It is a misfortune that Tagore's evaluation has been much affected by the relationship between India and Japan, and also by the rapid modernisation and Westernisation of Japan. The first contact was not at all successful and he was once almost forgotten.

However, translations continued with sincerity and we now have numerous works of Rabindranath Tagore in Japanese. As mentioned above, many of those translations were done from the original and we have at least reached the point when we can appreciate Tagore's works in the context of Indian literature. We can certainly be proud of this achievement, and should step forward to further study and evaluate Tagore as a poet of World Literature.

Notes:

1. Okakura Tenshin, whose real name is Okakura Kakuzo, was the author of the influential book *Ideals of the East* (1904). Okakura's visit and activities in India were recorded in *Tagore, Kakuzo Okakura*, 65–72. Yokoyama Taikan was a painter who created the new style of Japanese painting.

2. Mashino, 'Indo koshi', 43–52. There might have been a kind of confusion about the author at this point. Mashino's piece translates as 'Old poems of India,' but at the same time he clearly mentioned the name of the poet as 'Rabindranath Tagore of Bengal'.

3. Mashino, 'Shoka-no Tagoru-ron-ni tsuite', 13.

4. Uchigasaki, 'Yoju-no kage', 58–62.

5. In the article 'Tagoru to Indo-bunka', 2–9, he recollected the condition of those days.

6. Kora Tomi, a Christian, who played an active part in Rabindranath's later visits to Japan, said that she too had regularly read this magazine and came to know about Rabindranath.

7. Miura, *Shinrin tetsugaku; Sei-no jitsugen.*

8. Kimura, 'Tagoru shokan', 54.

9. Mashino, *Indo shinshishu Gitanjali.*

10. Miura, *Kada-no okurimono.* (Kada is the Japanese form of 'gatha' in Sanskrit.) It is, however, unclear on what ground Kimura Taiken criticised this title saying that it was 'not appropriate'.

11. Mashino, 'Futatabi Miura Kanzoshi-wo imashimu', 46–54. Miura, 'Bukkyoto Tagoru-no kokoro', 79.

12. Nakazawa, 'Beruguson to Tagoru', 60–77. Other than that, he wrote several articles and books on almost the same topic.

13. Ebu, *Tagoru-no shiso oyobi shukyo*, 1–2.

14. Uchigasaki, 'Tagoru-shi-o mukau', 154–5. This article was written before Rabindranath arrived, but published only after his arrival.

15. Iwano, 'Tagoru-shi-ni chokugen su', 7. This statement criticising Rabindranath was printed with his speech at the Tokyo Imperial University. *Asahi Shinbun*, which sponsored some of Rabindranath's speeches, reported on his visit favourably throughout. But we should note here that most other newspapers showed a rather indifferent attitude and sometimes did not report at all.

16. Hay, *Asian Ideas of East and West*, 6–7.

17. Inoue, 'Tagoru-no koen-ni tsuite,' 47–8.

18. Tanaka, 'Tagoru-shi-niataeteshinonihonkan-o ronzu', 292–3.

19. Ebina, 'Shijin Tagoru-no bunmei hihyo-o yomu', 20–1.

20. Ibid., 23–4.

21. Hay, *Asian Ideas of East and West*, 96.

22. Noguchi, 'Tagoa-wa hikkyo yomei gaku nomi', 5.

23. An interview with Noguchi Yonejiro, *Igirisu Bungaku* [English Literature], 1, no. 7 (June 1929), 30–3.

24. Kawahigashi, 'Tagoru-no insho,' 135. 'Waka' literally means Japanese poetry and refers to poems written in the classical style consisting of 5, 7, 5, 7 and 7 syllables in each line.

25. The reporter wrote about his meeting with Rabindranath as follows: "The poet seems very anxious [to know] if his idea of Pan-Asianism will be wholeheartedly accepted. I said "There will be no need to worry about such things. Most of the people in Japan agree with your view and they will be very happy if your visit is announced." The poet said, "I need some more invitations to impel me to go there." Tokyo *Asahi Shinbun*, 26 April 1924, 7.

26. Those new translations are: *Gisei* [*Sacrifice*] by Oda Ritsu, *Gora* [*Gora*] by Sano Jinnosuke, and *Unmei-no fune* [*The Wreck*] by Miyahara Koichi.

27. Sano, *Gora*, 9.

28. Ono, 'Tagoru-no 'Gora'-ni arawareta Indo-no fuan,' 106.

29. Noguchi claimed that "it is the war of "Asia for Asia" blaming Chiang Kai-shek as a puppet of the West. Letter from Noguchi to Rabindranath, 23 July 1938, cited in 'Poet to Poet', *The Visva-Bharati Quarterly*, 4, no. 3 (September 1938), 199. We can read the entire correspondence in the same magazine.

30. Noguchi, 'Mitabi Tagoru ni atau,' 278–9.

31. Later, Noguchi was strongly criticised for being a typical intellectual who cooperated with the war efforts and his name was almost erased from the history of modern poetry.

32. Yamamuro, 'Tagoru Shishu', 164.

33. Yamamuro published his translation of Tagore's poetry three times— in 1943, 1957 and 1966. The last one, in which the author added many new translations, has become the standard edition.

34. 'Tagoru', Tokyo, Tagorukinenkai, 1961.

35. Watanabe, 'Tagoru shishu', 3–5.

Works cited:

Azuma Kazuo. *Tagoru*. Tokyo: Kodansha, 1981.

— .*Tagoru*. Tokyo: Reitakudaigaku shuppankai, 2006.

Ebina Dansho. 'Shijin tagoru-no bunmei hihyo-o yomu' [Reading poet Tagore's criticism on civilisation]. *Shinjin*, 17, no. 7 (July 1916), 20–5.

Ebu Oson. *Tagoru-no shiso oyobi shukyo* [Tagore's Thoughts and Religion]. Tokyo: Nichigetsusha, 1915.

Hay, Stephen. *Asian Ideas of East and West*. Cambridge: Harvard University Press, 1970.

Inoue Tetsujiro. 'Tagoru-no koen-ni tsuite' [About the speech by Tagore]. *Shinjin*, 17, no. 7 (July 1916), 47–51

Iwano Homei. 'Tagoru-shi-ni chokugen su' [An appeal to Tagore]. *Yomiuri Shinbun*, 16–17 June 1916.

Kawahigashi Hekigoto. 'Tagoru-no insho' [The impression of Tagore]. *Nihon oyobi nihonjin*, May 1916, 135.

Kimura Taiken. 'Tagoru shokan' [Some thoughts on Tagore]. *Chuokoron*, 30, no. 5 (1 May 1915): 53–8.

Mashino Saburo. 'Shoka-no Tagoru-ron-ni tsuite' [About the articles on Tagore]. *Seikatsu to Geijutsu*, 2, no. 10 (June 1915), 2–14. .

—. 'Futatabi Miura Kanzoshi-wo imashimu' [To admonish Mr Miura Kanzo once again]. *Seikatsu to geijutsu*, 2, no. 9 (May 1915), 46–54.

Miura Kanzo. 'Bukkyoto Tagoru-no kokoro' [The Heart of Tagore as a Buddhist]. *ARS*, 1, no. 1 (April 1915), 78–90.

Nakazawa Rinsen. 'Tagoru to seiyo-no kojinshugi' [Tagore and Western Individualism]. *Chuokoron*, 30, no. 3 (March 1915), 49–54.

—. *Beruguson to Tagoru* [Bergson and Tagor]. Mitabungaku, 6, no. 8 (August 1915), 60–77.

—. *Tagoru to sei-no jitsugen* [Tagore and the Realisation of Life]. Tokyo: Shincho'sha, 1915.

Niwa Kyoko, *Tagoru*. Tokyo: Shimizushoin, 2011.

Noguchi Yonejiro. 'Tagoa-wa hikkyo yomei gaku nomi' [Tagore is after all a YangMing follower]. *Asahi Shinbun*, 15 March 1915.

—. Mitabi Tagoru ni atau' [Presenting my opinion to Tagore third time]. *Bungeishunju*, 16, no. 19 (November 1938), 216–23.

Okura Kunihiko et al. *Tagoru*. Tokyo: Tagoru kinenkai, 1961.

Ono Shinichiro. 'Tagoru-no 'Gora'-ni arawareta Indo-no fuan' [The uneasiness of India which is expressed in Tagore's 'Gora']. In *Bukkyo to gendai shiso*, 104-6.

Tokyo: Daiyakaku, 1925.

Tagore, Surendranath, 'Kakuzo Okakura.' *The Visva-Bharati Quarterly*, 2, no. 2 (1936–7), 65–72.

Tanaka Odo. 'Tagoru-shi-ni ataete shino nihonkan-o ronzu' [Discussion about Tagore's view on Japan]. In *Saiko geijutsuno taisei shosei*, 287–316. Tokyo: Tenyusha, 1920.

Uchigasaki Sakusaburo. 'Tagoru to Indo-bunka' [Tagore and Indian Culture]. *Rikugo Zasshi*, 35, no. 5 (May 1915), 2–9. -.

—. 'Tagoru-shi-o mukau' (Welcoming Tagore). *Rikugo Zasshi*, vol. 36, no. 6 (June1916), 154–5.

Rabindranath's works in translation:

Mashino Saburo, transl. *Indo koshi* [Old poems of India]. Zanboa, 3, no. 2 (February 1913), 43–52.

—, Transl. *Indo shinshishu Gitanjali* [New Indian poetry, Gitanjali]. Tokyo, Toundo shoten, 1915.

Miura Kanzo, transl. *Shinrin tetsugaku; sei-no jitsugen* [Philosophy of a Forest: Realisation of Life]. Tokyo: Genosha, 1915.

—, Transl. *Kada-no okurimono* [Offering of a Gatha]. Tokyo, Tobundo shoten, 1915.

Miyahara Koichiro. *Unmei-no fune* [*The Wreck*]. Tokyo: Daiichishuppan kyokai, 1924.

Morimoto Tatsuo, transl. *Tagoru shisei-no uta* [Poems of life and death by Tagore]. Tokyo: Ningento rekishisha, 2002.

Onishi Masayuki, transl. *Ie to sekai* [*Ghare Bairel/ The Home and the World*]. Tokyo, Daisanbunmeisha, 1986.

Osanai Kaoru, transl. *Yubinkyoku* [*The Post Office*]. Tokyo: Sekai dowataikei kankosha, 1924.

Oda Ritsu, transl. *Gisei* [*Sacrifice*]. Tokyo, Nihon dokushokai kaiho, 1924.

Sano Jinnosuke, transl. *Gora*. Tokyo, Daiyukaku, 1924.

Shiratori Shogo, transl. *Shingetsu* [*The Crescent Moon*). Tokyo: Isseido, 1924.

Uchigasaki Sakusaburo, transl. 'Yoju-no kage' [In the shade of a Banyan tree]. *Rikugo Zasshi*, 34, no. 2 (February 1914), 58–62.

Usuda Masayuki, transl. *Saigo-no shi* [*Sheser Kabita/ The Last Poem*]. Tokyo, Hokuseido, 2009.

Watanabe Shoko, transl. *Tagoru shishu* [Poetry of Tagore]. Tokyo: Iwanami shoten, 1977,

Yamamuro Shizuka, transl. *Tagoru Shishu* [Poetry of Tagore]. Tokyo: Kawaide shobo, 1943 (subsequent edns.: Tokyo: Kadokawa shoten, 1957; Tokyo: Yayoi shobo, 1966).

Collections:

Tagoru kessaku zenshu [Complete works of Tagore's masterpieces]. Tokyo: Bunseisha, 1915.

Tagoru chosakushu (Collection of Tagore's works). 8 vols. Tokyo: Apolonsha, 1959–61.

Tagoru chosakushu (Collection of Tagore's works). 12 vols. Tokyo: Daisanbunmeisha, 1981–93.

Rabindranath's Short Poems
with Reference to Japanese
'Haiku'

Rabindranath's first encounter with Japan is said to have happened when Kakuzo Okakura, who is also known as Tenshin Okakura, visited India in 1901. Okakura was attracted primarily by Swami Vivekananda and he intended to invite him to Japan. Unfortunately his plan did not realize, and instead, he got acquainted with Tagore family through Sister Nivedita, who was a disciple of Swami Vivekananda.

Since Okakura was a well-known expert of Art, he naturally intended to get in touch with other members of the family who were involved precisely in that field, rather than the literature. Prominent among them were obviously Surendranath or Abanindranath. However, since Rabindranath was also closely connected to that circle, he must have come to know Okakura right from the beginning, and might have acquired some fresh ideas of Japan through this contact. A few years later when he first met Okakura, he published three short poems thereafter in 1905, where he tried to use Japanese poetic style for the first time. Here are those three short verses:

সাগরতীরে
শোণিতমেঘে হল

নিশীথ অবশান।

পুবের পাখী
পুরব মহিমায়

শুনায় জয়গান।

On the shore
Of an ocean, night ended
Wrapping in a red cloud.
A bird from the east
Sings the song of Victory
To the glory of the Orient.

সহসীর বীর
দেখেছি কত তারি
করেছে জয়
দেখেনি তোমাসম
এমন ধীর
জয়ের ধ্বজা ধরি
স্তব্ধ হয়ে রয়।

I have seen
Brave heroes so many
Defeating enemies.
Never seen such calm
Equal to those of yours
Holding the flag of victory
And standing still.

গেরুয়া বাস করি
ধর্মগুরু
শিখিতে গিয়েছিল
তোমার দেশে
আজি সে শিখিবারে
কর্মনীতি
তোমার দ্বারে ধায়
শিষ্যবেশে।

Wearing the cloth
Dyed with red ochre
Preceptor of virtue
Went to your country
To teach. Today he
Runs up to your door
To learn the system of work
As a disciple.

Thakur, Rabindranath, 1905, *Japaner Prati* in *Bhandar,*
Ashar, p.12.

Apparently, these were written in praise of Japan's victory over Russia and hardly anyone can find the importance of these trifle poems considering the genius of the great poet. However, there is one point we should not overlook, which is the metre of these poems. Rabindranath himself explained it in an article confessing that those were written following the style of Japanese poetry, namely 'sedoka', 'choka', and 'imayo'; accordingly. 'sedoka' is the form of 5,7,7,5,7,7 syllables, 'choka' is the form of 5,7,5,7,5,7,7 (actually, one can continue 5, 7, as long as he/she wishes and only in the end must repeat 7 in this style), while 'imayo' is the form of 7,5,7,5,7,5,7,5. What we can see is, Rabindranath strictly followed the orders of each of those forms in 'Kalabritta'.

Actually, those were not popular styles of Japanese poetry of that time. 'sedoka' was the style which was often used in Nara period (A.D.710-84), while 'choka' also is an old style that can mostly be seen in 'Manyoshu' (the first collection of Japanese poetry of 7th and 8th century). Moreover, 'imayo' is not a poetic style, but a style for songs which was popular from the middle of Heian period (A.D.794-1192). It is not known where from or from whom Rabindranath acquired the knowledge of these forms. Anyway, it's worth mentioning that the most popular and typical Japanese poetry style after *Kokinwakashu* (another collection of Japanese poetry of the very beginning of 10th century) is 'tanka', which is composed with 5,7,5,7,7 syllables.

This 'Tanka' style is still widely used in Japanese poetry, and 'waka', meaning Japanese poetry, generally indicates 'tanka'. However, 'haiku' style poetry is worldwide known these days, rather than 'tanka'. 'haiku' is even shorter than 'tanka' and composed with only 5.7.5 syllables. It is important to note that 'haiku', though composed following the first three syllables of 'tanka', is not just a part or a shorter form that, despite the overtly similar form. 'haiku' has another root in literary history that distinguishes it from 'tanka'.

'Haiku's root is Renga which is a rather specific style of composing poems by several poets joining together. This style became popular during Muromachi period (1336-1573) . The first part of 'renga' is called *'hokku'*, and *'haiku'* is an independent form of *'hokku'*. One of the greatest *'haiku'* poets, Matsuo Basho (1644-94), was considered to be the founder of this style and Basho was originally an instructor of *'renga'* style of poetry. Rabindranath introduced two famous *'haiku'* of Matsuo Basho in his travelogue *Japan Yatri*.

Furuikeya
Kawazutobikomu
Ikeno-oto

পুরোনো পুকুর
ব্যাঙের লাফ
জলের শব্দ।

The ancient pond
A frog leaps in
The sound of the water.

Kareedani
Karasuno tomaritaruya
Akinokure

পচা ডাল
একটা কাক,
শরতকাল।

On a withered branch
A crow perched
Autumn evening.

(Here we followed the English way of writing 'haiku' in three lines. However, 'haiku' in Japanese is usually written in one single line)

Thakur, Rabindranath, 1919, *Japan Yatri*, Visva-Bharati, p.74-5.

These are probably the most well-known *'haiku' in* Japan and Rabindranath explains the meaning of two haikus in a rightful way. Moreover, he also discovers the essence of Japanese culture through poetry making and appreciates these poems in following words:

This tendency towards restraining self-expression is also reflected in their poetry. Nowhere in the world can three-line poems be found. These three lines are enough for both poets and their readers. That is why since I came here I have not heard anybody singing in the street. Their hearts do not gush like a stream, but stay still like the tranquil water in a lake. All their poems I have heard so far are visual poems and not songs. The heart's burning and complaints do spend up one's soul, and they have little expense in that. All their expression of inner feelings takes the shape of the sense of beauty.

Thakur, Rabindranath, 1919, *Japan Yatri*, Visvabharati, p.82.

This article, written in 1916 when Rabindranath first visited Japan, is probably the first proper introduction of 'haiku' to Bengali readers. This was about the time when European readers too, a few though, came in touch with this short form of poetry. Lafcadio Hearn (1850-1904), Paul-Louis Couchoud

(1879-1959) and Basil Hall Chamberlain (1850-1935) were the first generation of Westerners who introduced haiku to European readers. Especially, *Japanese Poetry* by Chamberlain (1910) was the first authentic introduction of Japanese poetry that included Basho and 'haiku'. Chamberlain stayed in Japan from 1873 to 1911 basically as an English language instructor. However, despite this highly acclaimed work on Japanese poetry, he was not appreciative of Japanese poems. Apart from Chamberlain, Hearn and Couchoud also translated some 'haiku' and it is well known that the Imagism movement in the West was also influenced by the concept of *Haiku*.

Mass popularity of 'haiku' is a post-World War II trend. It was Reginald Blyth, who also stayed in Japan for a long time; through his epoch making 1949 publication entitled 'haiku' triggered the sort of a boom of composing *Haiku* in other languages.

Rabindranath visited Japan during the time of the first stage of 'haiku's encounter with the world. His stay in Japan was rather short compared to those writers or scholars mentioned above and besides, he also did not know Japanese language at all. In that sense, it is rather surprising that he could describe the characteristics of the style so precisely in *Japan Yatri*, though he quoted only two 'haikus' and briefly described those in a short passage.

Here we encounter a very significant question; was Rabindranath himself influenced or inspired by 'haiku' in the same way as the followers of Imagism?

Talking about short poems, we can say without hesitations that even before coming to know about 'haiku' or any other forms of Japanese poetry, Rabindranath had a hand in writing short poems. He published *Kanika*, a collection of short poems, in 1899. He called those poems as 'epigrams'and said these are the same kind of poems that are called 'subhasita' in Sanskrit. Let us see some of his poems from *Kanika*.

কত বড় আমি নহে নকল হীরাটি
তাই তো সন্দেহ করি নহ ঠিক খাঁটি।

How big I am, imitated diamond says
That is why I doubt it is not the real.

দ্বার বন্ধ করে দিয়ে ভ্রমটারে রুখি।
সত্য বলে, আমি তবে কোথা দিয়ে ঢুকি?

Closing the door I shut out the wrong
Truth says then from where I can get into?

Thakur, Rabindranath, 1899, *Kanika,* Visvabharati, p.20,21.

Apparently, these are not serious poems but epigrams as the author mentions and he did not write any more short poems for many years except those we saw in the beginning.

Visit to Japan certainly inspired him to write short poems again, though different in style. *Stray Birds* in

1916 was an outcome of his visit to Japan and this little book of English short poems was received favorably all over the world. On the other hand, his collection of Bengali short poems titled *Lekhan* was published much later in 1927. This book was a photocopy version of his handwritten text, which is quite unusual for his works. In the preface he says, "Personal relationship will be lost in a printed book, but when I came to know there is a way of printing my handwriting, I decided to make this book". "Personal relationship" here indicates that many of those poems were written for people he met in Japan or in China. However, a basic question that arises here is, was it the only reason for the delay of the publication of *Lekhan*? Why he hesitated to publish short poems in Bengali, whereas those written in English were published straightaway? We can find a clue in an article written by him that I quote below.

When I was in China or Japan, almost every day, I had to respond to the request of writing something. In this way, I wrote so many poems on pieces of papers, on silk handkerchiefs or on folding fans. I was requested to write in Bengali letters so that they can observe my handwritings as well as the way of Bengali writings. While writing this way on many occasions here and there I got used to write two or three line poems and even discovered the joy in this kind of writing. This style, in which the poet has to condense and express one's thought in two or three lines without excessive words often became more precious to me than longer poems. I believe that we are so accustomed to read longer writings that we cannot accept a poem if it is short in length…

In Japan, no one considers short poems as something trifle. It is their wish to find something great in small because they are artists by nature. They cannot even imagine that someone might measure the beauty by length or weight. This is why I never hesitated to write two or four line poems. Few years before when I wrote songs of *Gitanjali,* many of the readers lamented over my disability of writing poetry and we can find quite a number of such readers even now.

Once my pen came to know the joy of writing this kind of short poetry, I opened my notebook even if there was no request; I began writing these poems following my heart's desire. And also, in order to melt readers' hearts, I wrote like the following one:

আমার লিখন ফুটি পথধীরে
ক্ষণিক কালের ফুলে,
চলিতে চলিতে দেখে যারা তারে
চলিতে চলিতে ভুলে।

My writing is a short-lived flower
That blooms on the roadside
People come and go getting a glimpse of it
And forget as they move forward.

But if you think about it, you will realize that he, who watches the flower while walking, is responsible for forgetting, not the short-lived flower..

Thakur, Rabindranath, 'Lekhan' in **Prabasi 28, 2,1** (*Kartik*, 1927), pp.453-4.

Here Rabindranath clearly proclaims the joy of writing short poems. Not only joy, he also claims that short poems are not inferior to longer poems. However, we can also feel his suspicion that those shall not be well accepted in the literary world of Bengal. It is rather surprising that even *Gitanjali*, which is no doubt one of the best collection of poetry in Bengal language, was once criticized because of its compactness. Anyway, this indication reminds us the fact that Bengali readers in general are fond of or accustomed to reading longer poems, at least in those days. This is maybe one of the reasons why Rabindranath hesitated to publish those poems in Bengali soon after writing. In the end of the article, he says "if you think about it, you will realize that he, who watches the flower while walking, is responsible for forgetting, not the short-lived flower." What he wanted to say here is that even if those short poems are ignored or not considered as proper poems, it is not the responsibility of the poet for that default, rather the responsibility of readers.

It has already been mentioned that Rabindranath had written short poems before his encounter with Japanese poetry. However, we should also remember that he had written those as 'epigrams' as claimed above. There is no doubt that he could discover the pure sense of poetry in 'haiku' while he stayed in Japan; and this discovery certainly made its way in his later short poems. Let us see some of the poems from *Lekhan*.

স্বপ্ন আমার জোনাকি
দীপ্ত প্রাণের মনিকা
স্তব্ধ আঁধার নিশীথে
উড়িছে আলোর কণিকা।

My dream is firefly
Shining jewel of life
In the still and dark night
Particle of light flies

যখন পথিক এলেম কুসুমবনে
শুধু আছে কুঁড়ি দুটি।
চলে যাব যবে, বসন্ত সমীরণে
কুসুম উঠিবে ফুটি।

When a traveler came to woods
There were only two buds
When he leaves, in the spring breeze
So many flowers bloom

Thakur, Rabindranath, 'Lekhan' in *Rabindra-Racanabali vol.14*, Visvabharati, p.159, 165.

These are, of course, not 'haiku', and here Rabindranath did not adopt Japanese poetry style either as he once did in 1905. Japanese poetry style is based on 5 and 7 syllables whereas Bengali is based upon 6 and 8 syllables. So it is easily taken for granted that Japanese poetry form does not primarily suit Bengali language. Anyway, if we read through all these poems, we can find poetical sense which is hardly seen in *Kanika* and hence it is reasonable to presume that the difference was brought by Japanese short poems, especially 'haiku'.

Yet, Rabindranath did not go on further in this path of poetry making. This is also natural considering his ability of composing poetry out of true nature of Bengali language. Moreover, his poetry is too richly melodious to be composed in such compact form. One more book of short poems of his was *Sphulinga* and this was the collection of short poems which were not included in *Lekhan*. *Sphulinga* was published in 1945 after Rabindranath passed away.

After one hundred years of Rabindranath's first comment on Basho's 'haiku', this form composing poems is now known and recognized throughout the world and many poets of different languages, including those of Bengali, are currently trying to compose 'haiku'. 'Haiku' is usually written in three lines in all other languages except Japanese. In English, many of those poems do not rigidly follow the form of 5,7,5 though it is recommended that one line should be under 5, 7, 5 syllables. There is another important rule in 'haiku' that is, 'kigo' which means words indicating a specific season. There are thousands of words in Japanese which indicate each of the four seasons and one must use one of them in 'haiku'. There is even a special dictionary for that purpose in Japan. This rule is all the more difficult to apply in other languages because each culture has separate concept of season.

On the other hand, there has also been a change in Japanese 'haiku' composition in modern time. Some *Haiku* poets started to write 'jiyuritsu haiku' meaning free style 'haiku', which has no 'kigo' and also do not follow the 5,7,5 form. Taneda Santoka (1882-1949) and Ozaki Hosai (1885-1926) were the most well-known and excellent *Haiku* poets of this kind; though the orthodox style still remains the main stream. But there is a question, what really 'haiku' is if they do not follow the rule. There is all the more confusion if we look around all those short poems written in various languages under the name of 'haiku'. This question, what is 'haiku' after all, is yet to be answered.

What is certain nowadays is that, Japanese 'haiku' poets cannot simply ignore those 'haiku' poems written in other languages, and this situation leads all poets to reconsider the real nature of 'haiku'. And it is also true that this kind of inter-cultural exchange inspires both sides of poetry making.

In Bengali 'haiku' we can find some examples which are written following exactly with 5, 7, 5 syllables. However, there is another and probably more serious problem with composing 'haiku' in Bengali. That is, what should be the meaning of syllables here? In other words, which meter should be adopted in 'haiku'- 'mishrabritta', 'kalabritta' or 'dalbritta'? Various trials can be seen in Bengali 'haiku', though not many of them are successfully composed with 5,7,5 syllables. Regarding 'kigo', I have not yet found any 'haiku' in Bengali which is conscious about it. But I believe, since Bengali literature is rich in seasonal expressions; poets of Bengal can easily apply the concept of 'kigo' in 'haiku' that they compose. In the first place, *Gitabitan* has headings depicting seasons and there we can see songs for spring, summer, or Rainy season etc.

I cannot say how far Bengali poets are to proceed in their trials of composing 'haiku' or similar style of poetry. However, there is no doubt that this kind of trial and cultural interchange will enrich Bengali literature itself. It is definitely fortunate for Bengali poets and readers that Rabindranath was the first poet who introduced Japanese short poems to the readership. It was not only the form of 'haiku' that he wanted to convey, he always looked into the deep inside of the culture as well. And what he eventually has described in *Japan Yatri* or in other writings is essentially the true spirit of Japanese poetry.

Rabindranath Tagore's
Message to Japan

1. *The Message of India to Japan*: What was his message?

Rabindranath Tagore visited Japan for the first time in 1916 and delivered a famous speech entitled 'The Message of India to Japan' on 11th June at the Imperial University of Tokyo, which is now known as the University of Tokyo. The presentation was a rather short one and it is worth reading through even today. Here, we are going to look briefly into his 'message.' In the beginning of the speech, Tagore openly expressed his surprise at Japan's sudden rise after Meiji Restoration, saying that "One morning the whole world looked up in surprise, when Japan broke through her walls of old habits in a night and came out triumphantly."

There is no flattery or irony here and he never hesitated to admit or admire what he believed to be true. This we can see in his assessment of Europe as well. Even under the condition of colonial subjugation, he did not hesitate to recognize its greatness by saying in the same speech that "I must not hesitate to acknowledge where Europe is great, for great she is without doubt." Still, naturally he could not help pointing out some of the evil sides of Europe as well.

> Europe is supremely good in her beneficence where her face is turned to all humanity; and Europe is supremely evil in her malefic aspect where her face is turned only upon her own interest, using all her power of greatness for ends which are against the infinite and the eternal in Man.

Here he is criticizing Europe, however, he is not condemning Europe only for its subjugation of India. He is claiming that it is "against the infinite and the eternal in Man". As we can see from this or other statements, Tagore is always concerned about the true dignity of human kind or individuals, not so much of a country's rise or ruin.

In this context, Tagore considered that Japan had a greater responsibility not only for Asia, but for the whole world.

> Of all countries in Asia, here in Japan you have the freedom to use the materials you have gathered from the West according to your genius and your need. You are fortunately not hampered from the outside, therefore your responsibility is all the greater, for in your voice Asia shall answer the questions that Europe has submitted to the conference of Man.

He urged Japan to answer the questions taking advantage of not being "hampered". But what are the questions? He says, the questions that Europe has submitted to the conference of Man, which means whole human being. These are not the questions that only Europe is concerned, not the questions Asia alone should respond to Europe. These are questions related to the welfare of all human kind and even Europe could not yet find the answer. Let us have look a bit more precisely into what Tagore intended to ask Japan to do.

The whole world waits to see what this great Eastern nation (Japan) is going to do with the opportunities and responsibilities she has accepted from the hands of the modern time. If it be a mere reproduction of the West, then the great expectation she has raised will remain unfulfilled. For there are *grave questions* that the Western civilization has presented before the world but not completely answered. The conflict between the individual and the state, labor and capital, the man and the woman; the conflict between the greed of material gain and the spiritual life of man, the organized selfishness of nations and the higher ideals of humanity; the conflict between all the ugly complexities inseparable from giant organizations of commerce and state and the natural instincts of man crying for simplicity and beauty and fullness of leisure, all these have to be brought to a harmony in a manner not yet dreamt of.

Here again he is talking about the "questions that the Western civilization has presented before the world". They are; "the conflict between the individual and the state, labor and capital, the man and the woman and so on. These questions are not yet, of course, answered even today. On the contrary, aren't we facing the same problems or witnessing that everything around is becoming much more complicated?

It may surprise us that he uses the word 'diversity' again and again in this speech, the word of which we have become aware of quite recently. He also says 'Man will have to respect differences', again, a concept that we advocate today more than ever before. As a result, what we need to observe here is that, Tagore's message is something transcending generations or time. In other words, it is timeless and universal.

In the end of the speech, he asks Japan once more to consider her responsibility that she may be able to carry out.

> Now the time has come when we must make the world problem our own problem; we must bring the spirit of our civilization into harmony with the history of all nations of the earth
>
> In this task of breaking the barrier and facing the world Japan has come out the first in the East. She has infused hope in the heart of all Asia. This hope provides the hidden fire which is needed for all works of creation. …For this we offer our thanks to this land of the rising sun and solemnly ask her to remember that she has the mission of the East to fulfill.

This was the message of Tagore to Japan. It might be too a heavy responsibility to ask for, but he dreamt that Japan, a fellow Asian country, would solve the problems by the wisdom of its own. There is nothing wrong about it and we should be rather honored to be asked to do so. However, surprisingly, most of the intellectuals of Japan of that time ignored the message, or rather had shown discontent with it. Why was that?

2. Reaction of Japanese intellectuals: Why wouldn't they listen to him sincerely?

It should be noted that there had already been to some extent a strain in the relations between the two countries, of which Tagore was most likely unaware of, and also a kind of apprehension that the Japanese people would not listen to Tagore's message unbiased, as we can see from the following comment, which was written by Uchigasaki Sakusaburo, a critic who translated some of Tagore's poems from English.

> The visit of the greatest poet born in modern India will be a great stimulus for us to take an interest in Indian thought. There is a tendency among the Japanese in general to ignore India's philosophical ideas because of the country's political subjugation, and thus to dismiss Tagore as one who has come from a ruined nation. This is a great loss for us.

Uchigasaki had written this article just before Tagore's arrival in Japan. According to his testimony, there was already an existing mood in the country that they wouldn't listen to poet's words, even *before* he was to say anything. Actually, there was a so called 'Tagore boom' in the previous year, and some critics reacted unfavorably to this sudden popularity. Some of them even ridiculed the great poet as 'a poet from a ruined nation'. Though ordinary Japanese had shown some degree of excitement over the visit, however, no such enthusiasm or even interest can be traced among the intellectuals right from the beginning. In this circumstance, some ignored Tagore's message, some irrationally reacted unfavorably, and some criticized Tagore without going through the speech carefully. Here is a comment made by a representative intellectual of those days.

> This might not have been the main point of his speech, but considering his attitude as a whole, I think it was one of condemnation of science.…What Japan is today is because we assimilated western civilization as our own. Western civilization is a creation of science. So if we reject science, we have to go backward in the course of history. …We are not wearing western civilization like a decoration piece on the surface.

This was written by Inoue Tetsujiro, professor of the University of Tokyo. He said he himself didn't go to listen to Tagore's speech like most other intellectuals who made comments on his speech. Actually, those people read the speech printed in the newspaper and made comments, but I doubt if they read it carefully enough.

There are misleading points in this statement that we cannot overlook. First of all, Tagore never condemned science itself. He only says "The real truth is that science is not man's nature, it is mere knowledge and training. By knowing the laws of the material universe, you do not change your deeper humanity" and nothing more. Also, he did not regard science in the same light as Western Civilization in the same manner as Inoue did. It is actually, as we all know, not as simple as that. Secondly, Tagore never described modern Japan as a country which only 'wears western civilization'. On the contrary, in the same speech he also says, "I cannot believe that Japan has become what she is by imitating the West."

Tagore's idea of East and West or of Asia was also not shared by Japanese intellectuals. Tagore naturally considered Japan as a member of Asia or the East, saying that "Japan, the child of Ancient East" or "She has her legacy of ancient culture from the East". However, many of Japanese intellectuals disagreed with this idea, as the following statement testifies.

> India is an old country and Japan is a comparatively new country. …India has many things to be proud of in her history, but Japan has hardly anything in her past and should rather have something she can be proud of in her present and future. …Considering her natural capacity for imbibing other civilizations, I would say that Japan's brothers are not China and India, but England and France. A classification of civilization cannot be easily made by its location.

This was written by a Christian priest Ebina Dansho and even he, who was exceptionally favorable to Tagore, could not share the idea of the East presented by Tagore. The message of Tagore failed to reach Japanese people as far as we examine articles that are still available.

3. *The Spirit of Japan*: The danger behind nationalism

Tagore delivered another speech entitled *The Spirit of Japan* on 3 July at Keio University. *The Message of India to Japan* was rather a humble request to Japan, however, in the next speech, he stepped into the more complex issue of the 'danger' hidden behind nationalism.

> What is dangerous for Japan is, not the imitation of the outer features of the West, but the acceptance of the motive force of Western nationalism as her own. Her social ideals are already showing signs of defeat at the hand of politics. I can see her motto, taken from science, "Survival of the Fittest," writ large at the entrance of her present-day history—the motto whose meaning is, "Help yourself, and never heed what it costs to others"; the motto of the blind man who only believes in what he can touch, because he cannot see.

Ebina, whose words are quoted above, is actually a rare intellectual, who has rather minor influence though, reacted to this warning of Tagore sincerely as he says:

> However, when the poet said with indignation that the motto of "the strong devouring the weak" must not be allowed in this East though it plays tyrant in the West, he struck a blow to the eagerness for territorial expansion by the Japanese. Those who are bent on such expansion, ridicule him by calling him 'a poet from a ruined nation'. But we should listen carefully to his words. If it were the time when Japan herself was apprehensive of

domination by the West, she would have sympathized with the poet. However, today people are no more afraid of being colonized and moreover they themselves are rather ready to attack and invade other nations economically or politically, there are many who naturally abuse the poet's words as ruinous.

These statements were made at the time of the 1st World War and it is natural for Tagore to reprove sharply the dark side of nationalism and Ebina was also right about the path Japan was gradually following. But if we read the passage of *The Spirit of Japan* once again, we can realize that what Tagore was warning about is not the specific phase of the time. I am sure many of us admit that we are still facing the same problem of nationalism today.

Considering the fact that even the earlier speech delivered at the University of Tokyo was not well accepted, we can expect that this second speech was all the more rejected. However, the truth is; there was no big reaction anymore; as if people lost interest in what he says.

Can we assume then that the words of Tagore came to nothing after all? We must not leap to that conclusion because the whole history of relationship between Tagore and Japan did not end at that point. However, we have to admit this first real encounter of the two did not have a successful finishing touch.

On the whole, the Japanese in general had been accepting Western culture and science, though often mixing up the two, quite positively and there was little chance of their sharing the image of materiastic West. Tagore's warning against militant imperialism was more or less out of tune with these people. Moreover, considering their country rather closer to the West than to the East, there was little inclination to think about Japan's role in Asia in the same way as the poet had defined it.

Still, we should not underestimate the influence of Tagore among the voiceless or less influential group of minorities. They crowded the hall every time where he delivered his speeches, and they listened to him eagerly. Even after adverse criticisms toward Tagore were expressed here and there, people still gathered to listen to him. The impression of the poet stayed long and deep in their minds and, because of that, Tagore was never completely forgotten during the dark era of war.

In 1924 and in 1929, Tagore visited Japan again, and we can find much smaller scale of reactions in newspapers and magazines. However, although the enthusiasm generated during his visit in 1916 was missing in 1920s, his lectures attracted many. In 1924, it was reported that more than two thousand people, mainly students, came to listen to his lecture at the University of Tokyo. In the same year, he also delivered a special lecture for women and, again, the hall was filled up by about two thousand women who came to listen to him.

4. Poetry and Songs of Tagore: Tagore's words will never vanish.

Some of you might have heard the name of Noguchi Yonejiro in the context of friendship with Tagore. It is in fact doubtful if there emerged a literary friendship in a true sense. Noguchi has never praised Tagore's poetical genius without reservation and has never taken the role to introduce him to Japanese literary world. Anyway, he tilted more and more towards Nationalistic ideas throughout the 1920s and 30s and finally contradicted in strong words Tagore's statement on the China-Japan war. Tagore was certainly shocked by Noguchi's refutation and there were a couple of letters exchanged between them on this subject, though neither was successful in convincing the other. Noguchi's reaction shows the atmosphere in Japan at that time that did not allow him to evaluate Tagore positively.

In this period of history, Tagore was considered to be an enemy or at least of supporting the enemy, and the mood to dismiss him became the primary focus. Poet and translator Yamamuro Shizuka offers an insight into the political setting of the era:

> I first published Tagore's poetry in 1943 and it was during the time Japan was at war. The inhumane war of aggression was being carried out. ...I intended to resist that, though I had little influence. That is why I translated the works reflecting such a profound love and humanity written by this great Asian poet. Tagore

was almost forgotten and ignored by then, since he was considered to be belonging to the enemy side; and despite such an adverse situation, an editor of Kawaide shobo dared to publish the book. However, a very strict censorship was imposed during the wartime, and twelve poems were expunged from the collection at the end.

It should be noted here that at the height of the war people like Yamamuro looked at the poet as a symbol of humanism and it was through his personal effort and the bold attempt taken by a publishing company that a new collection of poems came out. The spirit of Tagore did not totally vanish and it was silently handed down to the next generation.

After the last visit of Tagore in 1929, the impact of the poet gradually withered as we see above. Moreover, as Japan had taken the path of militarism, as predicted earlier by Tagore, even his name disappeared from public discourse. This uneasy situation was, however, completely overturned after the end of the war, and in the late 1950s we can see the emergence of a new trend of re-discovering Tagore. Yamamuro, quoted above, published a new edition of his translated poetry and others also joined this new tide of publications.

On the occasion of the Tagore centenary celebrations in 1961, several new translations appeared and a publishing company Apolonsha planned to issue an eight-volume collection of Tagore's works. The second volume never came out but the rest was published one by one and among those new translations, the most important work is definitely the complete translation of original Bengali *Gitanjali*. Actually, the first translation from Bengali language was done in 1929 by Sano Jinnosuke, who stayed in Santiniketan for several years and was recommended to translate *Gora* by the poet himself. Anyway, this was the first direct translation from Bengali poetry and later reissued in an Iwanami Shoten paperback series in 1977. A striking feature of the book is that Watanabe Shoko, who was a renowned scholar of Buddhism, translated not only all the poems of the original *Gitanjali,* but those of the English *Gitanjali* as well. He presented both translations in a single volume so that readers could compare and recognize clearly the fundamental differences between the two. Many readers today know that English *Gitanjali* is not the complete translation of Bengali *Gitanjali*. The poet omitted some of the poems of *Gitanjali* as well as he added quite a few from his other poetry collections. Watanabe pointed out that the English *Gitanjali*'was meant for English readers. He implied that Japanese readers can also esteem those poems which were excluded from the English version and he believed that this kind of appreciation would lead them to a real understanding of Tagore's works.

As we can see that through this unique effort of Watanabe the translation of Tagore's genius stepped into a new stage, that is, as direct translations from Bengali. The new generation of translators, who were involved in introducing Tagore from then on, all knew Bengali well and most of them were scholars of Indian studies. Two decades later in 1981, another collection of twelve-set volume started to be published and it has opened up the path to the appreciation of Tagore in the context of Indian literature.

In the light of this new appreciation of Tagore in Japan, two more small episode need to be added at the end. Kawabata Yasunari, Japan's Nobel laureate novelist, once delivered a lecture in 1969 quoting Tagore's words. There he said:

> Indian saint poet Rabindranath Tagore in his speech delivered in Japan says, "every race has a responsibility to present its identity to the world." He also said "Japan has brought forth its culture of a complete style, and developed its insight which can find truth in beauty and beauty in truth."

Kawabata was 17 years old in 1916 when Tagore first visited Japan, meaning that he was one of those voiceless young students at the time. Later he recollected that he saw the picture of Tagore in a newspaper which gave him an impression like a sage and he started reading his writings. As already mentioned, the younger generation including women who were excited most over the poet's visit and in spite of the negative attitude of renowned professors or critics of those days, these young people shared a positive impression of the poet and his words stayed long in their mind.

One more episode that should be added is about deliberate wrong perception of Tagore. In 1916, a critic and writer Iwano Homei criticized Tagore harshly in a number of papers and finally he spoke in dispraise of Tagore song without having any knowledge about what Tagore song is all about.

> I think it was just two years ago that you all of a sudden have become popular in our country. However, it was only because some of the publishers and translators tried to introduce something new for their personal gain. People with knowledge are hardly impressed by your poetry and your ideas.… I heard your poems are given melodies and they are sung in your country. I have also heard that you proudly sang your own songs in Kobe. But poems which can be accepted as music cannot be as good as pure poetry.

Iwano was always irrationally unfavorable to Tagore and this statement is also a kind of false accusation. Still, we have to admit it is not easy for us to understand what does Tagore song mean for Bengali people or how important it is to be a song, not just a modern style poetry, in the context of Bengali tradition of culture.

Recently one of my students was fascinated by Tagore song and made a film titled *Tagore Songs*. I was quite moved by the fact that after a lapse of more than a hundred year from the statement that Iwanno made, a young Japanese girl is trying to discover the true appeal of Tagore songs.

Appreciation or popularity of the poet can go up and down in the course of history, but we can always find something good, something valuable, something beautiful from our past. True, it was pity that Tagore and Japan's first encounter did not end up successfully and we should regret about that. But at the same time, we should not worry too much about it because we observe the fact that true words and true poetry will never vanish nor disappear.

Rabindranath Tagore And Japan:
His Visit With A Message And Its Outcome

Introduction

Rabindranath first visited Japan in 1916. As he carried along with him an 'Asian message' for Japan, the visit had a great significance in the history of Indo-Japan relationship in the modern era. Both India and Japan were busy imbibing western civilization after they had encountered the West in 19th century. On the other hand, there was no direct and strong relationship between these two Asian nations. As a result, it may not be wrong to regard this visit of Rabindranath as a great and rare opportunity that the two countries met directly as modern nations.

Thus we must appreciate its historical significance, however, at the same time; we must also admit that this opportunity did not provide any tangible success. It is a well known fact that the Japanese intellectuals reacted unfavorably to Rabindranath's 'message' and so a bridge could not be readily built. It was not easy largely because the meeting itself contained an inconsistency. Rabindranath had brought a message for the 'East' and the Japanese people welcomed him and listened to him anyway. However, what made this encounter all possible was the Nobel Prize, an award that he received from the West. Japan would probably never have discovered Rabindranath, the great poet of Bengal, should he not been given that authorization by the West.

Without the award Rabindranath could probably have never raised any controversy, and the distortion or the confusion surrounding his visit was in a way the natural outcome of this twisted situation. Yet, there are also some other causes that might have led this relationship between Rabindranath and Japan to the point of distortion or confusion and in this short paper, we would try to give a possible and convincing explanation to it.

1. Some questions on Stephen Hay's view

Among the studies done on this subject, *Asian Ideas of East and West* by Stephen Hay is probably the most exhaustive.[1] His main concern is to make clear the different ideas of 'East' that were presented by a number of intellectuals from India, China and Japan. However, he has placed Rabindranath at the centre of his study. He too has thoroughly examined the reaction to Rabindranath's interpretation of the East in Japan and has a considerable explanation for it.

Stephen Hay has summarized Rabindranath's visit in 1916 as follows:

> The next major thrust toward Asian unity was taken by India's leading poet, Rabindranath Tagore, who visited Japan in 1916 with the express purpose of propagating the idea of a renascent Eastern civilization. He was welcomed enthusiastically by Japan's educated class, not because of his friendship with their own Okakura, but because he had been awarded in 1913 one of Europe's highest accolades, the Nobel Prize for Literature. In three public

lectures, "India and Japan", "The message of India to Japan" and "The Spirit of Japan", Tagore presented his view of the Oriental civilization to which he assumed both countries belonged. Each Japanese intellectual reacted to Tagore's message in his own way, but when all their comments were published it was clear that most of them disagreed with the Indian poet's concept of a spiritual East standing aloof from, and defiled by, a materialistic West". [2]

This conclusion seems to be comprehensive and also a widely accepted one. However, we should re-examine it once more here since we believe there still is a gap between what had actually happened and "the fact" presented by Stephen Hay.

Our first question on 'the fact' here is: did Rabindranath clearly intend to propagate his message?

According to C.F. Andrews, Rabindranath had an expressed purpose of winning co-operation of China and Japan[3] and it was this view that had been assumed in all the studies so far. We cannot deny Andrews' testimony at all, but at the same time, it should be noted that we can scarcely find any such clear intention in Rabindranath's own writings, including his letters. He of course had had a desire to visit Japan even long before the visit could materialize. But his desire had been rather personal one, as he said in a letter, "Probably because I very much need the peace of some unknown, far away country, that this proposal of going to Japan or elsewhere comes back again and again despite all obstructions."[4] He also expressed the same desire in an interview that he gave after reaching Japan, as it had been reported, "his (Rabindranath's) habits were retired and solitary, and that he wished to be as free from public meetings during his visit as possible".[5] His first trip to Japan was in fact materialized all of a sudden by an invitation that he received from America. It may be misleading to consider that this visit was totally intended for the purpose of conveying his 'message' to Japan, though he delivered, after all, speeches to present his ideas with some eagerness.

Another question on Stephen Hay's conclusion above is: did Japanese intellectuals react to the message itself?

Stephen Hay says, "He (Rabindranath) was welcomed enthusiastically by Japan's educated class." But the fact was not as simple. True, there were certain educated people who welcomed him, but a greater number of intellectuals were indifferent right from the beginning. The rhetoric repeatedly used to disapprove of Rabindranath's ideas, such as "a poet from a ruined nation," had been already on circulation the year before and therefore, the indifference can be traced back to 1915, the time of the so-called 'Tagore boom'.

This 'Tagore boom' in 1915 was triggered by the awarding of Nobel Prize and a rumor of his visit to Japan. This sudden popularity had already raised some questions among intellectuals as we can observe in some articles comments like this: "It is difficult to say that his popularity so far in Japan was caused by a true understanding of Tagore and appreciation of him and the fascination." by Ebu Oson[6] or "After all, intellectuals of our country swallowed Rabindranath without examining and perhaps they will discharge it without digestion." By Kato Chocho.

Indeed, the 'Tagore boom' in the year before his visit did not help with understanding of Rabindranath's ideas. On the contrary, there was a kind of negative mood before they actually listened to any of his words, the mood such as "we have already known him and it's not worth listening to him seriously." It after all sounded as if Kato Chocho's prophecy; "they will discharge it without digestion"[7], coming true.

As Stephen Hay mentions the name of Okakura, we should also survey the relationship between the two here. Okakura (Okakura Kakuzo, or Tenshin, 1863-1913) was the first Japanese intellectual that Rabindranath came across and it is also likely that through Okakura Rabindranath got some information on Japanese culture. Actually 1901, the year in which Rabindranath's mentioning of Japan is tracing back to the farthest, was the year when Okakura first visited India and got in touch with Tagores. At the time Rabindranath was little known outside India and Okakura too was not famous outside Japan as the visit was made before the publication of *The Ideals of the East*[8] and the book was written during that first visit. Therefore, their friendship was established simply on their genuine appreciation for each other's natural gifts and character. Okakura might have influenced

Rabindranath and this possibility should not be ignored. Here influence does not mean the influence on the idea of the 'East', but also on the image of Japan which Rabindranath had been cherishing in his mind before his visit.

There is one point that we should consider in reference to Okakura. Though Rabindranath had taken him for a representative of Japan, after 1901, he was no more influential in Japan and did not commit himself to the stream of living Japanese culture as he had used to do before. He lived mainly outside Japan since then, and in a sense, was an outsider to Japan. Therefore he did not play any part in introducing Rabindranath to Japan, and except a small circle of painters, people even did not know there was a friendship between them.

There is also another important question that comes up in examining Stephen Hay's investigation. He has divided the Japanese intellectuals into two groups — one group westernized and exceptional, the other tradition-bound and orthodox. Here is what he said:

> The greatest irony in the reception of Tagore's idea of Asian spiritual revival by his fellow writers in Japan is that those who praised his message most warmly were men like Noguchi, who had been most deeply influenced by English and American Romantics, while those who condemned it most harshly were writers like Kawahigashi and Iwano, who were most deeply committed to the revival of Japanese traditions.[9]

There seems to be no doubt that Noguchi (Noguchi Yonejiro or Yone, 1875-1947) was a representative of 'westernized intellectuals' and the foremost admirer of Rabindranath. But if he was a real admirer of Rabindranath, how did he become an opponent on the controversy over the China-Japan war in his later years, as it is widely known? And furthermore, what are the implications of a Japanese or non-westerner to be westernized?

Noguchi was not indeed a simple admirer of Rabindranath as it is generally believed. He came to know Rabindranath in England soon after his poetry had made a great splash in Europe. However, it does not mean that Noguchi played an important role in introducing Rabindranath to Japan. He did not translate any of Rabindranath's poems before 1916. Instead, he wrote four articles on Rabindranath in 1915, but these were not entirely favorable to Rabindranath. Let us have a brief look at one of those articles written in 1915.

> At least I cannot find anything new and surprising in Rabindranath's philosophy. … In the East, at least in Japan, the value of Rabindranath is not as much as that in the West. The Western people that got in touch with Eastern thought only recently, must have found Rabindranath's ideas new and peculiar. However, we Japanese need to investigate our ancestors' efforts and distinguished works before we read Rabindranath's works.[10]

Here he does not evaluate Rabindranath's idea or philosophy and he did not change this opinion until the end as we can find almost the same view in his interview recorded in 1929.[11] This view of Noguchi is quite suggestive in the sense, this can be one of the reasons why people did not listen to Rabindranath's 'Asian message' seriously. Once he considered Rabindranath as an 'Asian' poet, he lost his earnest desire to know his philosophy or ideas regarding Rabindranath as one of those wise men he knew from the past. Indeed, this is one of the typical attitudes of Japanese intellectuals of the time.

Then how does Noguchi think about Rabindranath's poetry? The article below was also written in the same year, 1915.

> I do not know his original poems in Bengali, but as far as we can guess from the English translations, they can hardly be counted as prose poems … If we treat them purely as works of art irrespective of their philosophical background, then they do not have much value.[12]

Since there was no one in Japan who could appraise Rabindranath's original Bengali poetry, this evaluation of Noguchi based on English translations must have been quite definitive or influential. Of course there were some who disagreed with Noguchi's view appreciating highly Rabindranath's poetic emotion. However, the favorable appreciation of Rabindranath's works had never become dominant in the literary world of Japan ever since.

Apart from Noguchi, two other intellectuals had also been mentioned above by Stephen Hay, Kawahigashi Hekigoto (1873-1937) and Iwano Homei (1873-1920). True, there seems to be no doubt that being a 'waka' poet, Kawahigashi was a representative of tradition-bound poets. But again we must think over the position of 'waka' in the modern era. Did these modern 'waka'poets merely follow the style of 'waka' which had been continuously written from the ancient time? Were they not 'westernized' or did they not encounter any Western impact at all? They surely did. Indeed, Kawahigashi was one of those rare poets who actually listened to Rabindranath's speech. It is true that he did not approve his speeches on civilization, branding them too optimistic and unsatisfactory in the sense that they do not reflect the agony of Indian people. However, he was at the same time quite impressed by the way of Rabindranath's presentation.[13] On the whole, this was a typical impression of intellectuals of those days as we will see later, and we cannot say he 'condemned it most harshly.'

Iwano, the other intellectual mentioned by Stephen Hay, was a writer who had a rather peculiar position in the Japanese literary world and was not like Kawahigashi who mainly worked in the traditional mode, though not without a passionate programme for a self-styled revival. He was indeed one of the harshest critics of Rabindranath among Japanese intellectuals. But his criticism was not exactly a criticism of those speeches. He says:

I think it was only a year ago that you (Rabindranath) suddenly gained popularity. This was only because translators and publishing houses were trying to make money by introducing something new. We intellectuals were not really impressed by your poetry or philosophy since your ideas are very different from those of ours.[14]

This is a kind of emotional outburst came from the circumstance that surrounded Rabindranath and it was originally observed in the previous year. He simply held on to his attitude of rejecting Rabindranath since the time of 'Tagore boom' and he did not even bother to go to listen to the speeches. What he was irritated the most was the situation, say the welcoming party, the hosts surrounding Rabindranath or enthusiasm without actual comprehension, that is, the mood and attitude of Japanese people. Hence we should be careful when we analyze his comment as criticism directed toward Rabindranath's speeches and ideas.

It may not be wrong to classify Noguchi as westernized and Kawahigashi as tradition-bound intellectuals. But it becomes problematic if we consider Iwano too as a tradition-bound writer. He advocated naturalism when he started his career as a novelist, and then opposed to other naturalist writers declaring 'ichigenbyousha' (unifying description) or 'shinpiteki' 'hanjuushugi' (mystic half animalism). What he proclaimed was not always clear and logical, so that these were not widely accepted either. Anyway, it is difficult to place him in either of the sects that

Stephen Hay mentions. Furthermore, he criticized Rabindranath's speech by quoting Goethe, Baudelaire, and Wordsworth and so on, which means he disapproved Rabindranath's idea by applying Western standard.

It should be also reconsidered if those categories, westernized and tradition-bound, really reflected the typical reaction to Rabindranath. As we observed in the case of Noguchi and Kawahigashi, there seem to be some other factors behind the reaction irrespective of one favourable to Rabindranath or not.

Hence, there is a need focus again on Rabindranath's speeches and reaction to those speeches by Japanese intellectuals in an attempt to remain as much close to the fact possible.

2. 'The message of India to Japan'

C. F. Andrews, who accompanied Rabindranath on his visit to Japan in 1916, sums up his speeches and their reaction as follows:

> The people of Japan were impatiently waiting for the Poet's arrival in their own country. They received him with enthusiasm at first, as one who had brought honour to Asia.
>
> But when he spoke out strongly against the militant imperialism which he saw on every side in Japan and set forward in contrast his own ideal picture of the true meeting of East and West, with its vista of world brotherhood, the hint went abroad

that such "pacifist" teaching was a danger in war-time, and that the Indian poet represented a defeated nation. Therefore, almost as rapidly as the enthusiasm had arisen, it subsided.[15]

True, Rabindranath was called a poet 'represented a defeated nation' (more precisely, 'a poet from a ruined nation'). But this branding did not appear suddenly soon after his speech, as we have already mentioned. We can also observe the fact that most of the intellectuals were already indifferent when Rabindranath first visited Japan, that is, before he spoke out anything. Uchigasaki Sakusaburo (1877-1947, a critic), who was the earliest introducer of Rabindranath, lamented the situation as such saying:

> The visit of the greatest poet born in modern India will be a great stimulus for us to take an interest in Indian thought. There is a tendency among the Japanese in general to ignore India's philosophical ideas because of India's political subjugation, and thus to dismiss him as one who has came from a ruined nation. However, this is a great loss to us.[16]

This article was written just *before* Rabindranath arrived in Japan, and in such an atmosphere of conflicting attitudes, he delivered his speeches.

Rabindranath delivered three major speeches in 1916 as Stephen Hay says, *India and Japan, The Message of India to Japan* and *The Spirit of Japan*. Among those, *The message of India to Japan*, delivered on 11 June at Tokyo Imperial University, was the most influential, for a translation of the entire speech was published afterward in three newspapers and two magazines, so that all Japan could know what he had said. *Tokyo Asahi, Osaka Asahi* and *Jijishinpo* printed the translation on the following day. There was also a translation in the July issues of *Shinjin* and *Rikugo Zasshi*. Such extensive coverage was not seen in case of other speeches. Let us first review the speech briefly.

After expressing his reluctance to deliver such a speech, Rabindranath spoke of the image of Japan as follows:

> When things stood still like this, and we in Asia hypnotized ourselves into the belief that it could never by any possibility be otherwise, Japan has risen from her dreams, and in giant strides left centuries of inaction behind, overtaking the present time in its foremost goal. This has broken the spell under which we lay in torpor for ages, taking it to be the normal condition of certain races living in certain geographical limits. … And Japan, the child of the Ancient East, has also fearlessly claimed all the gifts of the modern age for herself. She has shown her bold spirit in breaking through the confinements of habits, useless accumulations of the lazy mind, seeking safety in its thrift and its lock and keys. Thus she has come in contact with an amazing eagerness and aptitude the responsibilities of modern civilization.[17]

And he turned his eyes also to Asia in general:

> Then fell the darkness of night upon all the lands of the East. The current of time seemed to stop at once, and Asia ceased to take any new food, finding

upon its own past, which is really feeding upon itself. The stillness seemed like death, and the great voice was silenced which sent forth messages of eternal truth that have saved man's life from pollution for generation, like the ocean of air that keeps the earth sweet, ever cleansing its impurities.

But life has its sleep, its periods of inactivity, when it loses its movements takes no new food, living upon its past storage.[18]

Here comes the issue of a mission that Japan must have for Asia, and this seemed to be his main thought, for he repeated it again and again in this speech. For instance he said:

Of all the countries in Asia, here in Japan you have the freedom to use the materials you have gathered from the West according to your genius and your need. You are fortunately not hampered from the outside; therefore your responsibility is all the greater, for in your voice Asia shall answer the questions that Europe has submitted to the conference of Man. In your land the experiments will be carried on by which the east will change the aspects of the modern civilization.[19]

Along with this, he voiced his critique of western materialism. He said that he did not hesitate to admit the greatness of the West, but there was also an evil side of western civilization:

Only there, where Europe is too consciously busy in building up her power, defying her deeper nature and mocking it, she is heaping up her iniquities to the sky crying for God's vengeance and spreading the infection of ugliness, physical and moral, over the face of the earth with her heartless commerce heedlessly outraging man's sense of the beautiful and the good.[20]

With a final exhortation, as it were, of the responsibility of Japan, he concluded this speech with following words:

> Eastern Asia has been pursuing its own path, evolving its own civilization which was not political but social, not predatory and mechanically efficient, but spiritual and based upon all the varied and deeper relations of humanity. ... In this task breaking the barrier and facing the world Japan has come out the first in the East. She has infused hope in the heart of all Asia. This hope provides the hidden fire which is needed for all works of creation.
>
> Asia now feels that she must prove her life by producing living work, she must not lie passively dormant, or feebly imitate the west, in the infatuation of fear or flattery. For this we offer our thanks to this land of the rising sun and solemnly ask her to remember that she has the mission of the East to fulfill.[21]

On the whole, in this speech he expressed doubts about western civilization and emphasized Japan's mission in her own East.

We have already observed the indifferent attitude of Japanese intellectuals toward Rabindranath and it means there remained only a small chance of building a meaningful relationship based on mutual trust between Rabindranath and Japan. Still, there were some who responded positively to Rabindranath's idea of Asia and civilization, irrespective of the circumstances. Here we are going to survey those rather 'exceptional' responses together with the 'typical' response from representative intellectuals of the time.

3. Japanese reactions

Obseving a number of unfavourable comments on Rabindranath and his speech such as that of Iwano as we have seen above, Nagayo Yoshiro (1888-1961), a writer, was firmly opposed to such criticism and such facile dismissal of Rabindranath. Nagayo had not shown any interest in Rabindranth before his visit, and had no role in either introducing or extending favor to him. But now it seemed he could not help interfering:

> Reading the newspapers, I felt that the people criticize Tagore thoughtlessly ... I think they have an attitude similar to that of arrogant rioters whose only purpose is to destroy idols. The attitudes of Iwano is the meanest of all ... We should listen with sympathy to the appeal that Rabindranath makes to us. And I think most people should pay him their respect for that. ... Tagore is being easily dismissed by some partly applaud him so easily. Tagore is the one who is suffering most. ... However, his visit is a kind of stimulus to Japan. There has been no such foreigner who had given us this chance to rethink. This is the result of his concern for Japan. He is different from other visitors in this matter.[22]

Nagayo appreciated Rabindranath's eanest concern for Japan saying he is the first who gave Japan a chance to rethink. It is rather pity that taking a step forward, he did not respond to Rabindranath's idea itself. He is appealing here to his fellow writers who are unjust to Rabindranth. However, it does not bring by itself any positive reaction to Rabindranath's message.

Nagayo belonged to the literary group named 'Shirakaba'. This group published a literary magazine named 'Shirakaba (white birch), and all the members were students or graduates of Gakushuin University, which used to be the institute for the children of aristocratic class only. Apart from Nagayo, some other members of this group also showed sympathy towards Rabindranath, though again, it is not that they really responded to Rabindranath's 'message' positively.

Here is another statement by Arishima Takero (1878-1923, a novelist), who belonged to the same group. He did not at all oppose Rabindranath, but at the same time, he could not help feeling antipathy to the circumstances surrounding the poet.

> I have spent my time until today without reading any of Tagore's original work or article about him since I have had an antipathy to him caused by thoughtless recommendations and instigations. I know it cannot justify my ignorance. However, this is certainly an unpleasant fact that Tagore was never noticed before getting the Nobel Prize, and that he has come to our view only after that. I wish the day will come when we would be able to get the taste his works with a calmer heart.[23]

This is a typical attitude of writers and poets of the time, irrespective of whether westernized or not, staying away from the controversy, remaining calm or rather cold, having a slight antipathy without reading any of Rabindranath's works.

Akita Ujaku (1883-1962 a playwright), was a rare intellectual of the literary world who had shown more positive attitude towards Rabindranath since he heard both the speeches, *The Message of India to Japan* and *The Spirit of Japan* and also, visited Rabindranath personally. He did not write much about it, but many years later recollecting memories of the time he said:

> I have attended both of his speeches at the Tokyo Imperial University and the Keio University. … However I could not agree with his idea of dividing civilization into two, the spiritual one and the material one. …On 11 July, we visited Tagore at Hara's house in Yokohama. I do not remember now what we asked him and what he said in reply.[24]

His impression of Rabindranath seemed to have faded with time and we may say that Rabindranath's visit did not after all leave a great impact on him. Still, it should be noted that he still remembered Rabindranath talking about two civilizations, the spiritual East and the material West, and made clear of his disagreement with this idea.

Not only Akita, but others too were hesitant in accepting Rabindranath's idea of two civilizations. Ebina Dansho, a Christian priest, though he was one of those 'exceptional' intellectuals who were favorable to Rabindranath, did not agree with Rabindranath's idea of East and West, and expressed his view in following words:

> India is an old country and Japan is a comparatively new country. ... India has many things in history to be proud of, whereas Japan has hardly anything of her past and should rather have something she can be proud of in her present and future. Japan has never been exhausted and asleep under the burden of her ancient civilization. ... Considering her natural capacity for imbibing other civilization, I would say that Japan's brothers are not China and India, but England and France. A classification of civilization cannot be easily made by its location.[25]

This statement draws our attention since it shows how he, and maybe other Japanese too, thought about his own country. He said Japan has almost nothing in her past and rather should be proud of her present and future. What he is proud of is not ancient Japan which had closer tie with China or India, but a modern Japan that looks similar to England or France. His image of Japan or the East does not overlap with that of Rabindranath.

Still, he did not totally disapprove Rabindranath's idea, or rather; he did appreciate Rabindranath as was evident from the following description:

> However, when the poet said with indignation that the motto of "the strong eating the weak" must not be allowed in the East though it plays havoc in

the west, it came as a great warning to the Japanese in their eagerness for territorial expansion. Those who are bent on such expansion ridicule him by calling him "a poet from a ruined nation." But we should listen carefully to his words. When Japan herself was apprehensive of domination by the West, she would have sympathized with the poet. However, today when people are no more afraid of invasion and moreover, when they are themselves rather ready to attack and invade other nations economically or politically, there naturally are many who abuse the poet's words as "ruinous".[26]

This statement is important not only because Ebina appreciated Rabindranath's humanism, but also because he admitted the rise of a militant nationalism in Japan. His statement deserves greater attention because he gave possible explanation as to why Rabindranath's words were rejected. It is true that both India and Japan had faced a cultural crisis when they had met the West. But the question is, did they face it in the same way? Besides, had not Japan face it earlier and fully tided it over by the time Rabindranath on the scene? Few more comments need to be quoted to get a clear understanding.

Tanaka Odo (1868-1932), a philosopher and a critic, wrote an article on Rabindranath's speech titled *Tagorushini ataete shino nihonkan o ronzu* (Offering Mr. Tagore my opinion of his views on Japan). Tanaka learned Pragmatism from John Dewy at Chicago University and later became a professor at Waseda University. As a result, he can be counted as one of the 'westernized' intellectuals, but never been favourable to Rabindranath. Here is what he said:

> When there was no political unity in Japan, no readiness in the Japanese army, when our ancestors were enjoying peace, then suddenly, as if it was a bolt from the blue, those three or four nations of the West, visited them and threatened them. ... Our ancestors were told by those nations that they must choose either death or modern civilization. And they had chosen modern civilization as the only way to escape death. The death which they feared was not physical death but the death of the spirit. What they feared most was yielding to violence or the loss of their independent existence. ... There was only one motive in our adoption of western civilization and commencement of modernization. That motive, of course, was to maintain our independence against fears of oppression by foreign countries.[27]

He says "Our ancestors were told by those nations that they must choose either death or modern civilization." and modern civilization here, of course, means western civilization. He, and most probably other Japanese too, had an idea that there was no question about adopting western civilization in order to survive as an independent nation, and therefore, we must say, there was little tendency to reconsider the evil side of 'materialistic' west.

Towards the end of the same article, Tanaka quoted a sentence from Rabindranath's [The East with her ideals, in whose bosoms are stored the ages of sunlight and silence of stars, can patiently wait till the West,

hurrying after the expedient, loses breath and stops]
and commented: "This is a too easy and carefree
comment."

We would like to quote here one more article which
is basically similar to that of Tanaka, but more authentic
and more influential. The author is Inoue Tetsujiro
(1856-1944), a philosopher and a professor of Tokyo
Imperial University. As an expert of German philosophy,
he too was a 'westernized' type of intellectual who
had spent 7 years in Germany in his youth and
introduced many of the western philosophical thoughts
and ideas. He was also one of the translators who had
translated poems for the book 'Shintaishisho' (Poetry
of new style), which was the first attempt in Japan to
translate renowned western poetry into Japanese and
which also became a source of modern poetry making
in Japan. However, he has never showed any interest
in Rabindranath and he did not seem to read any of
the writings of Rabindranath, at least seriously. He had
only written about his impression after the speech *The
Message of India to Japan* was delivered and here is what
he said:

> This might not have been the main point of his
> speech, but considering his attitude as a whole, I
> think it was one of condemnation of science. At
> least his followers, I am afraid, will believe it to be
> so. If this notion gains in strength then I fear that it
> may undermine our civilization or weaken our
> resolve to uphold it. ... What Japan is today is
> because we assimilated western civilization as our

own. Western civilization is a creation of science. So if we reject science, we have to go backward in the course of history. It may be all right to reject science in one's personal life, but it will be quite dangerous to do so as a nation.... We are not wearing western civilization like a decoration on the surface. It has gone deep into our psyche and has become the flesh and blood of Japan.[28]

He often wrote articles with the purpose of enlightening people, and here too we notice the same spirit. We may, therefore, consider that this expression of his is not as much to respond to Rabindranath himself as much it is to appeal to Japanese people.

In that same article, he also said that Rabindranath was from a 'ruined nation', and was in his speech, 'denouncing civilization.' He tried to refute that denunciation by saying "Especially we, as the people of a rising nation, should banish such Indian notions as pessimism or the weariness of life." Hence, once again, it is not a direct response to Rabindranth's speech, and all the more, this is not that he reacted to what Rabindranath said about Japan's mission. He further says:

Japanese intellectuals have already noted the points on which Rabindranath warned the Japanese. Irrespective of what he says, we will carry out what we think the best.[29]

With or without precise reading of Rabindranath's words, he did not take seriously Rabindranath's repeated appeal for Japan's mission or responsibility.

What Rabindranath suggested in his speeches was left behind in the rushing stream of Japan's history.

It is evident from these comments that Japanese people at the time cherished highly their independence as a nation. As Inoue and Tanaka said, they believed that they could maintain it because they had adopted western civilization or science so skillfully. They did not have any apprehensions about the impact of science; on the contrary they accepted it as beneficial to them.

Actually, this was the turning point when Japan was getting rid of the fear of foreign rule or of a cultural crisis. As a result it was at that time that Japan was also turning aggressive and drumming up the so-called nationalism. However, except for Ebina's statement quoted above, we find no article which echoed Rabindranath's fear of militant nationalism. There were some who supported or appreciated Rabindranath as a person who told them the truth. But the question of nationalism itself, which Rabindranath talked of again and again in his speeches, was not discussed.

It is not true, therefore, that Japanese intellectuals were as such repelled by his speech *The Message of India to Japan*. There did prevail in Japan a mood that could not but reject him. We should rather say that his speeches could not attract those that had already turned indifferent.

It should also be noted here that many of those who had later written articles criticizing his speeches, admitted that they had not gone to listen to those speeches. They had only read about the speeches in newspapers and recorded their objection. On the other hand, the newspapers always reported that "The speech was successful," "The hall was full of people" and so on. Those who did attend the meetings have also mentioned that it was difficult to get a ticket. So here, another question that comes up is: who then went to listen to Rabindranath? Considering the fact that most of the intellectuals said that they did not go, and still a lot of people went, we have to admit that most of the listeners were ordinary citizens or students who did not have any access to the media to ventilate their opinion. Also considering much enlightening statements as that by Inoue, it can again be safely assumed that Rabindranath must have enjoyed the popularity among ordinary people. It is difficult to ascertain their response since there is no document available except the fact that the attendance was indeed quite large. But we should also not ignore the importance of this faceless crowd.

4. Conclusion

We have observed the fact that many of intellectuals, irrespective of whether they were 'westernized' or not, were reluctant to respond in any way to Rabindranath's 'message', and even in the case of those who had responded, most of them reacted unfavourably. Here we confront another important question: who then were the people who supported Rabindranath?

We have already mentioned neither Okakura nor Noguchi had any role in introducing Rabindranath to Japan. Those who introduced him and translated his works in the early stage were people like Uchigasaki Sakusaburo, Miura Kanzo (1883-1960), Yoshida Genjiro (1886-1956) and Mashino Saburo (1889-1916). Mashino was a minor poet who unfortunately died before Rabindranath visited Japan. He tried his best in translating Rabindranath's poems from English until his untimely death. The other three were all associated with the magazine *Rikugo Zasshi*, which was published for young Christians and which always allocated a number of pages to Rabindranath. In fact, this group of Christians was most favourable to Rabindranath and the Christian priest Ebina Dansho who had been quoted above was also a member of the group. Naruse Jinzo (1858-1919) was another such intellectual who supported Rabindranath, though he did not really join the controversy over Rabindranath. Being a Christian priest, he studied in the United States and afterwards founded Japan Women's University. It was he who invited Rabindranath to the summer house of the University in Karuizawa to deliver speeches to students.

There were in fact a certain number people who were favourable to Rabindranath, but they were always minorities in Japan. Minority does not mean a few in numbers, but those who do not have any firm basis in Japanese mainstream, like Christians, young students or women. In Japan, being 'westernized' did not mean exceptional, as we could see from the example of those like Inoue or Tanaka, who were 'westernized' enough in the eye of ordinary Japanese, yet had a firm position in the mainstream and were also influential. On the contrary, Christians like Ebina or Uchigasaki were definitely well educated, but much less influential.

On the whole, Japanese intellectual mainstream rejected Rabindranath, but not exactly because what he had said, but mainly because of the circumstances surrounding Rabindranath, such as the way of introduction or the enthusiasm among ordinary people. In such a situation, Rabindranath failed to attract these intellectuals by his speeches. And even the small number of intellectuals like Akita or Ebina who were most favorable to Rabindranath, they too neither could share Rabindranath's ideas on civilization, nor agree with his classification of East and West.

Japanese in general had been accepting western culture and science almost positively and there was little opportunity to share the image of the dark and agree over the sphere of influence of the materialistic West. Thus, Rabindranath's warning over a militant imperialism was more or less out of the sight of those people. Moreover, considering herself closer to western countries rather than the East, there was little room to think about Japan's responsibility in Asia in line with what Rabindranath had said.

Then, can we conclude that the message of Rabindranath or relation between Rabindranath and

Japan came to nothing after all? The answer is partly yes and partly no. Of course it can be hardly said his visit to Japan was a success. We even cannot be sure of if there were some among the numerous 'minorities' on whom Rabindranath could in fact exert an impact. The young students who crowded the hall where Rabindranath delivered his speeches must have been largely involved in the militant nationalism in their later days. However, there is no clue if some of them ever remembered what Rabindranath had said to them in their youth.

However, we at least can see what was really happening in Japan in the course of history through Rabindranath's eyes and also can find out what people in Japan saw in Rabindranath, the act that actually reflected what they had in their mind.

This is still by far a long way from reaching the point in Japan when it can be said that we re-discovered Rabindranath and his speeches. However, it is still possible to find trace back the reality whenever we go back to the time of 1916 and open the pages of the scene. And we believe that it is never too late to find out the truth.

Notes:

1) Stephen Hay, *Asian Ideas of East and West* (Cambridge: Harvard University Press, 1970).

2) ibid., 6-7.

3) C.F.Andrews, *Letters to a Friend* (London: Allen and Unwin, 1928), 57-8.

4) Letter from Rabindranath to Rathindranath, 18, July, 1915, in *Chithi Patra 2* (Kolkata: Visvabharati, 1942), 33.

5) 'Sir Rabindranath Tagore in Japan,' *The Modern Review,* 20, no.2 (August, 1916) : 230.

6) Ebu Oson, *Tagoru no shiso oyobi shukyo* (Tagore's thoughts and religion), (Tokyo: Nichigetsusha, 1915), 1-2.

7) Kato Chocho, 'Tagoru ryuko ni taisuru fuman' (My dissatisfaction with the Tagore boom), *Yomiuri shinbun*, 15-18, May, 1915.

8) Okakura Kakuzo, *The Ideal of the East* (London: John Murry Co., 1903).

9) Stephen Hay, *Asian Ideas of East and West*, 96.

10) Noguchi Yonejiro, 'Tagoa wa hikkyo yomei gaku nomi' (Tagore is after all a Yang-Ming follower), *Asahi shinbun*, 15, March, 1915.

11) An Interview with Noguchi Yonejiro, *Igirisu Bungaku*, 1, no.7 (June 1929) : 30-33.

12) Noguchi Yonejiro, 'Sanbunshika to shiteno Tagoru' (Tagore as a writer of prose poems), *Chuokoron,* 30, no.5, (May, 1915): 68.

13) Kawahigashi Hekigoto, 'Tagoruno Insho' (The impression of Tagore), *Nihon Oyobi Nihonjin,* (May, 1916) : 135.

14) Iwano Homei, 'Tagoru shini chokugen su', (An appeal to Tagore), *Yomiuri shinbun,* 16-7, June, 1916.

15) C. F. Andrews, *Letters to a Friend* (London: George Allen & Unwin Ltd., 1928) , 68.

16) Uchigasaki Sakusaburo, 'Tagoru o mukau' (Welcoming Tagore), *Rikugo Zasshi*, 36, no.6 (Jun 1916) : 154-55.

17) Rabindranath Tagore, *The Message of India to Japan: A Lecture by Sir Rabindranath Tagore Delivered at the Imperial University of Tokyo* (Tokyo: Tokyo University Press, 1916), .1-2, 5.

18) ibid., 2-3.

19) ibid., 10-11.

20) ibid., 20.

21) ibid., 21-22.

22) Nagayo Yoshiro, 'Rokugo nite' (on the previous issue), *Shirakaba*, 7, no.7 (July 1916) : 101-2.

23) Arishima Takero, 'Ikani tagoruo miruka' (How I regard Tagore), *Shincho,* 23, no.7 (July, 1916) : 3-4.

24) Akita Ujaku, *Ujaku jiden* (Autobiography of Ujaku) (Tokyo: Shinhyoronsha, 1953), 56-7.

25) Ebina Dansho, 'Shijin tagoruno bunmei hihyo o yomu' (Reading poet Tagore's cultural criticism), *Shinjin,* 17, no.7 (July, 1916) : 20-21.

26) ibid., 23-4.

27) Tanaka Odo, 'Tagorushini ataete shino nihonkan o ronzu' (Discussion about Tagore's view on Japan), *Saiko Geijutsunotaisei shosei* (Tokyo: Tenyusha, 1920), 292-3.

28) Inoue Tetsujiro, 'Tagorushino koenni tsuite' (About the speech by Tagore), *Rikugo Zasshi,* 36, no.7 (1, July, 1916): p47-8.

29) ibid., 47.

All the translations from Bengali and Japanese are mine.

Rabindranath Tagore
And
Noguchi Yonejiro

Noguchi Yonejiro, a poet of Japan, is widely known as an admirer of Rabindranath. On the other hand, the controversy between Rabindranath and Noguchi over China-Japan war is also well known and this fact gives us the impression that Noguchi, who was once an admirer of Rabindranath, abruptly turned into a narrow-minded nationalist who's opposing to Raindrranath. If it is true, what was the exact cause of this Noguchi's inconsistency? And after all, what kind of friendship or relationship existed between these two poets? In this short paper, we will try to trace the real relationship between the two and find out the cause of inconsistency of Noguchi.

Noguchi was born in 1875. In 1891, he was admitted to Keio Gijuku which was not yet graded a university and studied English literature. He went to the United States in 1893 at the age of nineteen, and stayed there for nine years. He started his life there as a newsboy on a San Francisco Newspaper and soon after became a reporter. In 1895, he met a famous poet of the time, Joaquin Miller who allowed him to stay with him. In his cottage at Oakland, California, Noguchi started writing English poetry. His poems were first printed in the magazine *The Lark* in 1896 and his first book of poems *Seen and Unseen* was also published the same year. Though there was some adverse criticism, his poetry was on the whole favourably received. He published a few other books soon and his reputation was fairly established.[1] However, he was not satisfied with this success and decided to go to

England. In 1902, he left the United States and arrived in London at the end of the year. In the following year, he published another book of poems titled *From the Eastern Sea*, which established his fame in England. He finally returned to Japan in 1904 after 11years of absence. Immediately on return, he was appointed a professor of English literature at the Keio Gijuku which had by then been upgraded to a university. He stayed in this post until his retirement at the age of seventy.

In Japan, in spite of his reputation overseas he had hardly been accepted as an eminent poet. He was only known as a poet who had been successful in the United States and England. After returning home, he published poems in Japanese, but these were his own translations from his English poems. He had never written poetry directly in Japanese till the later years of his life.[2] It should be noted here that in Japan it is quite rare to write in English, and there has hardly been anyone except Noguchi who has written English verse. This can be safely assumed to be the reason why his place in the Japanese literary world was rather peculiar. Indeed, Noguchi was never fully accepted as a poet. He is still remembered only because he was well known outside Japan, not because his works were widely read or highly appreciated within the country. It was almost inevitable that his poetry, which was second-hand being a translation from his own English, was not estimated highly. And poems which were written directly in Japanese in his later years also did not gain much appreciation. Hagiwara Sakutaro who was certainly a representative poet of the time described Noguchi's *Hyosho Jojoshi*, which was published in 1923 at the age of fifty, as follows:

> What I felt first when I read Noguchi's poems was this – his selection of a topic or his way of conveying an idea or his use of poetic words, and more than these, his basic sentiment itself was not at all that of a Japanese. I felt as if I was reading a direct translation from the works of some Western writers.[3]

Considering that the mainstream of Japanese literature ignored Noguchi, this article by Hagiwara was still a rather favourable one. He admitted the value of his Japanese poetry explaining his peculiar situation in the Japanese literary world. We will quote more from this article later.

Noguchi went to England once again in 1914 to give some lectures on Japanese literature at Oxford University. There he first heard of Rabindranath and sent him a letter the following year after returning home:

> I was so often told of you while I was in London some months ago; how often I thought of you, and wished to know your personality. Now I am at home again, and still more think of you. Herewith I send you some books of my poems; will you read them?
>
> I had seen so many of your English friends in London,— Yeats, Ezra Pound and others.[4]

It is clear that Noguchi knew of Rabindranath before Rabindranath's first visit to Japan in 1916. However, it does not mean that Noguchi played an important part in introducing Rabindranth to Japan. He did not translate any of Rabindranath's poems before 1916.[5] Instead, he wrote four articles on Rabindranath in 1915. However, these are not entirely favourable to Rabindranath.

Among these, let us have a brief look first at *Tagoa wa hikkyo Yomei gaku nomi* (Tagore is after all a Yang-Ming follower). He expressed doubt regarding the value of Rabindranath's thoughts comparing them with those of O Yomei.[6] He said that there was nothing new in Rabindranath's philosophy especially for those who knew the Oriental philosophies. At the end of the article he concluded:

> At least I cannot find anything new and surprising in Rabindranath's philosophy. If Rabindranath was awarded the Nobel Prize for his philosophy, what kind of prize should a philosopher like O Yomei have been awarded? In the East, at least in Japan, the value of Rabindranath is not as much as that in the West. The Western people that got in touch with Eastern thought only recently, must have found Rabindranath's ideas new and peculiar. However, we Japanese need to investigate our ancestors' efforts and distinguished works before we read Rabindranth's works.[7]

As far as we can see from this article, Noguchi was in a way discouraging the Japanese people from reading Rabindranath's works closely.

In another article by him, 'Shijin to shite no Ta-sensee no kachi' (The value of Tagore as a poet), Noguchi talked of Rabindranath's style of poetry. He evaluates Rabindranath's English poetry as follows:

> The poetic prose he used in his *Gitanjali* and other poetry, is of the style that many people have used starting from the *Silence of Amour* by William Sharp. Therefore, this style is well-accepted in England and it is easy to be highly appreciated with it. I think that Tagore is enjoying his popularity largely because of this style of his poems.[8]

Noguchi was himself a poet successful in America and in England; so it was not unnatural for him to feel a kind of rivalry. It seemed difficult for him to praise Rabindranath straightaway, and indeed, we can hardly find any words of praise in these articles. Instead, we can trace a complexity in his explanation of Rabindranath's ideas and style.

In the following year, in 1916, their first meeting took place on the occasion of Rabindranath's first visit to Japan. When Rabindranath was on his way to Tokyo, Noguchi also got on the train and had a talk with him for the first time.

Noguchi reported their first meeting in the following words:

> Our conversation on the train naturally started with remarks about our common friends who are English poets. I said to him, borrowing Yeat's words, "your visit to London encouraged English men who were in doubt whether one could really

return to Chaucer's age when people had literary conscience. In the same way your visit to Japan has a significant meaning for us.[9]

Their meeting must have been a pleasant one. However, it cannot yet be concluded that Noguchi withdrew his criticism of Rabindranath and became an admirer of him until we take a look at his article on Rabindranath which was written immediately after.

In 1916, he sent an article to *The Modern Review* entitled *Tagore in Japan*. In this article he first admitted their– his and Rabindranath's– similarity as follows:

> As I already expressed somewhere, I returned home from London, let me say again much dissatisfied with the Western life founded on individualism and often egoism or self-satisfaction; in fact, I returned to Japan, whose spiritual safety should require her to refuse the western invasion with its long arms reaching out after exciting luxury or disruptive sensation. … He was evidently in the same thought.[10]

And he informs his readers about Rabindranath's speeches which were delivered in Japan and sums up:

> What Sir Rabindranath brought to the well-balanced intellectual Japanese mind was this: How can we properly check the Western invasion? Again how can we keep our own beauty and strength grown from the soil a thousand years old and let them realize the fullness of their nature, not curtailing all that is best and true in them at the threatened encroachment of foreign elements? After all he only presents this great momentous question; and like

any other prophet, he does not answer the question; only pointing the way by his inspired hand unseen but sure; it is our work to solve it.[11]

He explains here the meaning of Rabindranath's speeches and seems to evaluate them. However, we cannot be sure if this opinion is based on his true understanding of Rabindranath's speeches. At least he did not go to listen to them and there is no trace that he discussed those subjects with Rabindranath. Noguchi met Rabindranath only for a short while and read those speeches afterwards when those were published in the papers.

There was a big controversy over his speeches in 1916 among Japanese intellectuals. The majority criticized Rabindranath at that time, though there were still some who spoke in his favour. In his article of *The Modern Review*, Noguchi refers to these speeches as if he supported Rabindranath. However in 1916, except the one of *The Modern Review* which was published outside Japan, he did not publish any article in Japan on the speeches. That means he did not join the controversy at that time. This fact again shows his complex situation and mind which I try to explain later.

Though he did not give his opinion on Rabindranath's speeches, he did not maintain complete silence in 1916. He dedicated an English poem 'To Sir Rabindranath Tagore' in *Mita bungaku,* and reported on their conversation on the train, 'Tagoru-shi to kataru' (A talk with Tagore) in *Bunsho Sekai,* and discussed Rabindranath's short stories in

'Tanpenshosetsuka to shiteno Tagoru' (Tagore as a short story writer) in *Mita Bungaku*. In the last article, he gave his views on Rabindranath as follows:

> Rabindranath does not have any great value as it was once said in Japan, but at the same time, it is not true that he is totally insignificant as it is being said now in Japan. I myself am an admirer of Tagore and still sometimes read his works.[12]

Here he admits that he is an admirer of Rabindranath, but still his admiration is mixed with a considerable degree of criticism.

Whether he was an admirer of Rabindranath or not, he did not play an important part in creating a condition for the proper appreciation of Rabindranath at this stage. This is obvious from the fact that though he did not participate in the controversy over the speeches which were actually a turning point in Rabindranath's reception in Japan, he was equivocal in his judgment on Rabindranath's philosophy and poetry.

Just after Rabindranath's arrival the second time in 1924, Noguchi published an article 'Tagoru kitaru' (Tagore has come). In this article he explains Rabindranath's excellence as follows:

> He is a prophet who has the power to lead people and to show them a new wide world. He is a man who speaks for the future, and who explains things that are inevitable in our life. ... There are some critics who say that one cannot be a poet without background of philosophy. I myself believe that one can be a poet either with or without

philosophy, but Tagore is certainly a philosopher in many ways.[13]

Here he talks of Rabindranath's value as a prophet or a philosopher, but in the later part of the article he emphasizes the value of his poetry.

> His poetry is never queer or unnatural. In one word they are themselves art which does not allow any further argument. He is a poet who has a mission. If one sees only one phase of him, one may think that the mission alone is his concern. However, he has a strong tie with his people. Actually and naturally his voice sings songs of others though he may not have intended that. I believe this is why his works have such a value.[14]

Here he talks more sympathetic way than 1916. Noguchi who once did not see any significance of Rabindranath's philosophy or did not quite appreciate the style of his poetry, now admits his value as a prophet and a poet. Let us take a look at another article written in 1924.

> We have no prophets in Japan. We have no poets who will show us the way with a new philosophy. Stop saying Tagore is old fashioned. Stop saying there is nothing new in his philosophy or poetry. ... My belief is not always the same as Rabindranath's, but I am one who respects his efforts through poetry, prose and speeches to hark us back to original nature to build up a new life. ... I do not accept all of Tagore, but I strongly believe that he can be a force to rescue modern Japan.[15]

Though Noguchi now emphasizes Rabindranath's value, we still sense a lack of persuasion in him since there is an inconsistency when he declares "Stop saying there is nothing new in his philosophy or poetry." Was he not the one who used to say the same thing? It also reduces his credibility when he again and again mentions that he does not always agree with Rabindranath without pointing out the actual points of disagreement. Therefore, though these later articles have a favourable note not seen around 1916, we still cannot say that Noguchi is whole-heartedly praising Rabidranath.

> In 1924, Noguchi met Rabindranath again. He visited Rabindranath at the Imperial Hotel just after his arrival in Tokyo. At this time, Rabindranath mainly talked about his school at Santiniketan and discussed his future plans such as exchanging teachers between India and Japan.[16]

In 1929, at the time of Rabindranath's third visit to Japan, Noguchi agreed to be interviewed by the magazine *Igirisu bungaku* (English literature) and talked about Rabindranath. Here he spoke frankly about Rabindranath's ideas and works. First of all he was asked what he thought of Rabindranath as a poet. He said:

> He fixes his eyes on something beyond the real. And we should respect his message to create a new life by expressing a true love for life. However there is nothing original about this; a number of poets in history have expressed the same thoughts. His

Gitanjali which brought him such fame, proved to be his trump card, and he uses his tramp card quite effectively.[17]

And being asked about Rabindranath's ideas he stated:

> They seem to be something like Emerson's. In the East, he is someone like O Yomei.[18]

And lastly, when he was asked if he had listened to Rabindranath's lecture, 'Yukan tetsugaku' (The philosophy of leisure) which was delivered in 1929, he replied:

> I have not listened to it. So I do not know his philosophy of leisure, but I do not think it was anything very new. There are so many in the history of mankind who have found a philosophy of leisure.[19]

Here again he mentions the name of O Yomei and says that there is nothing new about Rabindranath's ideas. Though he published some articles that favourable to Rabindranath in 1924, his attitude basically did not seem to have changed since 1915.

As mentioned above, Noguchi started writing poetry directly in Japanese from 1922. In 1925 appeared a book of selected Japanese poems by him, 'Hyosho jojoshi'. A study of his poetry too, *Noguchi Yonejiro ron* (A study of Noguchi Yonejiro) by Hagiwara Sakutaro was published in 1929. In this article, Hagiwara said that there were certain things one should learn from Noguchi admitting his peculiar situation. He explained Noguchi's poetry in following terms:

According to the Westerners, the poetry of Noguchi is representative of the typical Japanese sentiments. However, in the eyes of the Japanese, his sentiments are those of the non-Japanese. … On the whole, Noguchi Yonejiro is one-hundred-percent a foreigner. … I think that the great gap between Eastern and Western civilizations is well proved by these mutually opposed views on Noguchi. The same person is stated to be "too much westernized" from the one side, and "a perfect Oriental" from the other. …

Noguchi as a poet reveals his ultra-nationalist sentiments and criticizes the confused and vulgar taste of modern Japan which is becoming westernized. His essays are exciting and are full of his passion as a poet, but his way of reasoning is inconsistent. … He himself is a foreigner by nature, and he writes poetry according to the grammar of a foreign language and thinks like a foreigner. Contrary to the nature of his, nay, because of this nature, in the field of ideas, he demonstrates his ultra-nationalism lamenting over the westernization of Japan.[20]

Hagiwara talked of Noguchi's delicate situation in Japan as also of his complex mind. It is a significant indication that the very reason behind his ultra-nationalism was his nature which had become very westernized. Noguchi, indeed, must have felt the conflict of identity since several times he expressed in his poetry his tragedy of not belonging to either society the Eastern or the Western. Noguchi says:

When a Japanese reads my Japanese poems, he says
"Your Japanese poems are not good enough, but
I guess your English poems are good."
When a westerner reads my English poems, he says
"They are not worth reading, but
I guess your Japanese poems are splendid."
To tell the truth
I am not confident of either English or Japanese
I am a double national
The tragedy is that I can be neither a Japanese nor a
Westerner.[21]

My home is not here.
I cannot but feel that
there is a suitable home for me
Somewhere else.[22]

In 1935, Noguchi visited Rabindranath at
Santiniketan. Though he stayed there only one night,
29 November, he was welcomed warmly and there
were some functions for him. Immediately after his
arrival at Santiniketan, he had a talk with Rabindranath.
At this meeting, Rabindranath said answering
Noguchi's questions; "My respect and love for the
Japanese people has never been reduced since I saw
them the first time. Especially, there are no women
who can be compared with the Japanese women."
Noguchi looked around the school and also met
Nandalal Bose and Kshitimohan Sen.

There was a formal reception for Noguchi on 30
November. Rabindranath welcomed Noguchi with
words such as: "At last the poet has come, the poet

who is the true messenger of the spirit of his people representing the culture which is national, but above all universal and of all time."[23] Answering this message, Noguchi gave a brief speech mainly about the nature of Japanese art. He spoke of Japanese poets and poetry as follows:

> I thank Japanese poets of the past for giving me this little natural world, from which I am able to step into a larger world. The real poetry, whatever it be, is but a little gate of mystery through which we go into a world of Eternity complete and round. … I know the western people would take the majority of the so called "flowering seven grasses" only for weeds. Remembering how our Japanese poets in the past discovered their beauty, I cannot but be thankful for that poetical service.[24]

I have mentioned above that Noguchi started writing in English in his youth and that in 1922, at the age of 49, he wrote some verses directly in Japanese for the first time. Since then he seemed to be inclined towards pure Japanese culture and art, as we can see from the fact that he concentrated on Ukiyoe or Japanese fine arts, especially for a period of ten years from 1926. In his speech at Santiniketan too, he emphasized the peculiarity of Japanese culture.

After returning home, Noguchi sent several poems and essays to *The Visvabharati Quarterly,* among which one was on Sharaku, a famous Ukiyoe painter.

Whatever his inclination was, his visit to Santiniketan was to renew his friendship with

Rabindranath. After returning home, he wrote a letter of gratitude, and in return Rabindranath sent a copy of his *Collected Poems and Plays* published by Macmillan.

In another letter, Rabindranath spoke of his hope to visit Japan again, but, he said, "the chances of its realization do seem remote; you would not of course understand my difficulties, for you have yet a quarter of a century to reach my age."[25]

In 1937, Noguchi published a book of English poems, *Ganges Calls Me*, apparently, the fruit of his trip to India. Naturally, he sent it to Rabindranath who answered in praising words.

This friendship was suddenly blown off by the explosive China-Japan war. Even before Rabindranath's letter acknowledged the receipt of Noguchi's book *Ganges Calls Me,* Noguchi took up the pen shocked by Rabindranath's statement on the China-Japan war.[26] In his first letter on this matter, he describes the war like this:

> But if you take the present war in China for the criminal outcome of Japan's surrender to the West, you are wrong because, not being a slaughtering madness, it is I believe, the inevitable means, terrible it is though, for establishing a new great world in the Asiatic continent, where the "Principle of live-and-let-live" has to be realized. Believe me, it is the war of "Asia for Asia".[27]

And then he emphasizes the extent of 'Sacrifice' on the side of Japan:

Borrowing from other countries neither money nor blood, Japan is undertaking this tremendous work single handed and alone. ... Putting expenditure out of the question, we are determined to use up our last cent for the final victory that would ensure in the future a great peace of many hundred years.[28]

And again he explains the purpose of the war, concretely this time:

Our enemy is only the Koumingtung government, a miserable puppet of the West. ... Chiang (Chiang Kai-Shek) is a living example who sold his country to the West for nothing and smashed his skin with the crime of westernization. Dear Rabindranath, what will you say about this Chian Kai-Shek?[29]

Rabindranath was certainly astonished at Noguchi's refutation. In his reply to the letter above he explains why he condemns Japan:

When you speak, therefore, of "the inevitable means, terrible it is though, for establishing a new great world in the Asiatic continent" – signifying, I suppose the bombing on Chinese women and children and the decoration of ancient temples and universities as a means of saving China for Asia – you are ascribing to humanity a way of life which is not even inevitable among the animals and would certainly not apply to the East, in spite of its occasional aberrations. You are building your conception of Asia which would be raised on a tower of skulls. I have, as you rightly point out, believed in the message of Asia, but I never dreamt that this message could be identified with deeds which brought exaltation to the heart of Tamerlane at his terrible efficiency in manslaughter.[30]

At the end of the letter he describes China together with Ciang Kai-Shek as follows:

> China is unconquerable, her civilization, under the dauntless leadership of Chiang Kai-Shek, is displaying marvelous resources: the desperate loyalty of her peoples, united as never before, is creating ever before the meaning of the enthuseiasm with which the big-hearted Japanese thinker Okakura assured me that China is great.[31]

Again Noguchi replied. In his next letter, we can see no change in his opinion. Starting with "No one in Japan denies the greatness of China," he again explains the war in the same manner:

> And nobody in Japan ever dreams that we can conquer China. What Japan is doing in China, it is only, as I already said, to correct the mistaken idea of Chian Kai-Shek.[32]

He says that there is a lot of mischievous propaganda which deliberately misleads people against Japan, and expresses his doubt regarding the source of Rabindranath's information on China:

> I hope that you will let me apply your accusation of Japanese astucity to China, just as it is. Seeing no astucity in China, you are speaking about her as an innocent country. I expected something impartial from a poet.[33]

Noguchi stuck to his opinion and continued to speak for Japan at times in an emotional tone, probably because, in his words, he "belongs to one of the responsible parties of the conflict." Once more, Rabindranath replied to his letter. Both the statements ran parallel without answering each other as Rabindranath himself admitted in his last letter:

> It seems to me that it is futile for either of us to try to convince the other since your faith in the infallible right of Japan to bully other Asiatic nations into line with your Government's policy is not shared by me, and my faith that patriotism which claims the right to bring to the altar of its country the 'Sacrifice' of other people's rights and happiness will endanger rather than strengthen the foundation of any great civilization, is sneered at by you as the "quiescence of a spiritual vagabond."[34]

Immediately after this controversy, Noguchi published an article in Japan titled 'Mitabi Tagoru ni atau' (Presenting my opinion to Tagore third time) explaining his point of view. He says:

> What I am afraid of is to be called a betrayer by my fellow countrymen. My belief, contrary to your belief, is that I want to be a true man before I am a poet. Therefore, it is important to me that I belong to a sovereign Japan. ... He (Romain Rolland) is a lucky man who can lead a comfortable life at the side of Geneva lake even after betraying his country. ... I do not have my Geneva, and I cannot let my family be starved to death. ... I do

not want to be a betrayer to my country even if I become a betrayer to intellectuals.[35]

He shows a strong sense of nationalism as expected from that statement of Hagiwara's given above. Noguchi had to show an ultranationalism because he felt an outsider in Japan. If he had been an ordinary Japanese poet, he would not have felt such a strong apprehension that he might be called a betrayer. However, Rabindranath naturally did not realize this predicament of Noguchi's. He had described Noguchi as "the poet who is the true messenger or the spirit of his people representing the culture which is national, but above all universal and of all time." Rabindranath had thought that he was a typical representative of Japanese intellectuals. But in fact, he was only an outsider and just because of that he could not be a nationalist and a universalist at the same time. In a sense, this controversy between Rabindranath and Noguchi was inevitable.

The argument came to an end without mutual agreement. Three years after that, that is 1941, Rabindranath passed away. Just after his death, a memorial service was held at Zojoji temple in Japan. On this occasion, while giving a speech on Rabindranath, Noguchi recollected the above controversy and said:

I thought he would understand my patriotic sentiment. I tried to assert that this temporary violence should be forgiven because this would help rebuild the whole East, explaining that Japan was rescuing the East from the West's fangs. Against this statement, Rabindranath only poured his idealism against use of weapons and described Japan as an aggressor without seeing the fact that this was the inevitable course of history. And he praised Chiang without knowing that Chiang was a puppet of the West. I could not help feeling sad for India, seeing that Rabindranath ironically accepted the exploitation of the East by the West. I have learned much from Rabindranath's idealism and even now I believe that there is no doubt about the eternal value of his ideas. … We were both born in the East, and our friendship lasted for thirty years though we were not completely frank with each other. The argument which broke the ties of our friendship was a sad incident for both of us.[36]

Even before this argument, Noguchi had said repeatedly that he did not always share Rabindranath's ideas. But he never made it clear on what points he differed with Rabindranath. The difference came to light at the very last stage of their relationship. And this gap was not made up till the end.

Noguchi is generally known as an admirer of Rabindranath. However, having studied his essays on Rabindranath, it seems difficult to say that he was ever an admirer in a true sense. Though he wrote a number of essays on Rabindranath, it cannot be said that he provided a consistent point of view for the benefit of the Japanese to evaluate Rabindranath, since his essays were more or less equivocal.

Noguchi was certainly one of the very few

intellectuals of Japan who made friends with Rabindranath. It was 'a sad incident' in Noguchi's words that their relationship was blown off in the end. But after examining Noguchi's life story, we must say that their relationship was quite delicate from the beginning. Rabindranath would never know the complexity of Noguchi's mind and situation in Japan. However, there is a possibility that Rabindranath had in a way sensed its brittle friendship intuitively since he also never praised Noguchi whole heartedly. The speech which was delivered on the occasion of Noguchi's visit to Santiniketan was almost the only one comment on Noguchi by Rabindranath and those words sound a little official than personal.

The tragedy is, Noguchi was always under the pressure that he must prove his identity. It was not that easy to get over the national identity for him and without getting over the situation, it was not possible to realize the true meaning of Rabindranath's message. And again, it is also not that easy for all of us today, in Japan or any other world outside Bengal, to overcome the wall which Noguchi had faced. There is no doubt Rabindranath was a great poet. But the true understanding of this greatness also requires a great effort. Misunderstandings and entanglements are everywhere when someone or something spreads beyond 'The Nation'. We must correct these one by one and come closer to true Rabindranath.

Notes:

1) These were *The Voice of the Valley* (1897), *The American Diary of a Japanese Girl* (1901), and *The American Letters of a Japanese Parlor-maid* (1902).

2) In the preface to *Chinmoku no chishio* which was published in 1922 at the age of forty nine, he himself said, "This was the first time I wrote poems directly in Japanese".

3) Hagiwara Sakutaro, 'Noguchi Yonejiro ron' (A study of Noguchi Yonejiro), in *Shiron to Kanso* (Tokyo: shiroto shisha, 1929), 206. Translation mine.

4) Letter from Noguchi to Rabindranath, 5 February 1915, now in the Rabindra Bhavana Archives at Santiniketan.

5) Throughout his life, Noguchi made only one set of translations of Rabindranath's poems in 1924; 'Bengarugo no shi' (Poems of Bengali language), *Kaizo*, 6, no.7 (July 1924): 1-14. Despite of the title, this is not a translation from original Bengali. He translated some poems from English.

6) O Yomei; Wang Yang-ming (1472-1529) Chinese philosopher and government official, led the revolt against the Neo-Confucianism.

7) Noguchi Yonejiro, 'Tagoa wa hikkyo yomei gaku nomi' (Tagore is after all a Yang-Ming follower), *Tokyo Asahi Shinbun*, 15 March 1915. Tranlation mine.

8) Noguchi Yonejiro, 'Shijin to shite no Ta-senss no kachi' (The value of Tagore as a poet), *Tokyo Asahi shinbun,* 30 March 1915. Translation mine.

9) Noguchi Yonejiro, 'Tagoru shi to kataru' (A talk with Tagore), *Bunshosekai,* 11, no.7 (July 1916): 205. Translation mine.

10) Noguchi Yonejiro, *Tagore in Japan, The Modern Review,* 20, no.5 (November 1916): 528.

11) ibid., 529.

12) Noguchi Yonejiro, 'Tanpen shosetsuka toshiteno Tagoru', *Mita Bungaku*, 7, no.5 (May 1916): 118. Translation mine.

13) Noguchi Yonejiro, 'Tagoru kitaru', *Yomiuri shinbun*, 5-8 June 1924. Translation mine.

14) ibid.

15) Noguchi Yonejiro, 'Tagoru no insho' (The impression of Tagore), in *Noguchi Yonejiro booklet 23* (Tokyo: Daiichi shobo, 1926), 32-4. Translation mine.

16) However, this plan did not materialize.

17) 'Tagoru zatsuwa' (Talk about Tagore) in *Igirisu Bungaku* (English literature), 1, no.7 (June 1929): 31. Translation mine.

18) ibid., 32. Translation mine.

19) ibid., 33. Translation mine.

20) Hagiwara Sakutaro, 'Noguchi Yonejiro ron', in *Shiron to kanso.* (Tokyo: Shirotosha shoten, 1929), 211, 221. Translation mine.

21) Noguchi Yonejiro, 'Jo' (preface), in *Nijugokusekisha no shi* (Poems by one with a duel nationality) (Tokyo: Genbunsha, 1921), 1-2. Translation mine.

22) Noguchi Yonejiro, 'Sakamichi' (A slope), *Nihon shijin*, 5, no.4 (April 1925): 4-5. Translation mine.

23) 'Noguchi at Santiniketan', *Visvabharati News*, 4, no.6 (December 1935): 45.

24) ibid., 46.

25) Letter from Rabindranath to Noguchi, 16 August 1938, now in the Rabindra Bhavana Archives.

26) "Your neibouring nation (Japan) which is largely indebted should naturally cultivate your cultural wealth and therefore should naturally cultivate your comradeship for its own ultimate benefit, has suddenly developed a virulent infection of imperialistic rapacity imported from the West and turned the great chance of building the bulwark of a noble destiny in the

East into a dismal disaster." *Visva-Bharati News*, 7, no.1 (July 1938): 3.

27) Letter from Noguchi to Rabindranath, 23 July 1938, "Poet to Poet", *The Visva-Bharati Quarterly*, 4, no.3 (September 1938): 199.

28) ibid., 199-200.

29) ibid., 200-1.

30) Letter from Rabindranath to Noguchi, 1 September 1938, ibid., 203.

31) ibid., 205.

32) Letter from Noguchi to Rabindranath, 2 October 1938, ibid., 206.

33) ibid., 207.

34) Letter from Rabindranath to Noguchi, 29 October 1938, ibid., 210.

35) Noguchi Yonejiro, 'Mitabi Tagoru ni atau' (Presenting my opinion to Tagore third time), *Bungeshunju,* 16, no.19 (November, 1938): 218, 221. Translation mine.

36) Noguchi Yonejiro, 'Tagoru tsuito no ji' (The memorial address on Tagore), in *Tateyo Indo* (Tokyo: Shogakukan, 1942), 278-9. Translation mine.

Translating Poetry

Introduction

Translating poetry is certainly a bold attempt since poetry is always trying to escape from a general meaning or function of sentences and it often depends upon images which are too unpredictable for foreign readers. Poetry is also very much dependent on the sound or language structure itself which is again not able to reflect in another language. However, these barriers did not always discourage translators who were attracted to the novel and fascinating images or expressions of foreign poetry. Indeed, like any other country, in Japan too, there appeared many outstanding works of translations which stimulated poets themselves and led them to a new kind of creation or even transformed the view of not only poets but also general readers and in the end transformed even the stream of poetry.

Before reaching such an extraordinary stage caused by a certain translation, needless to say, there are a lot of difficulties in the way that translators have to get over. In this small paper, I will first trace the introduction and translation of Rabindranath's poetry into Japanese and then will observe some of the excellent works of translation in the literary history of Japan in order to derive a future perspective of a certain achievement. In the context, I am also going to look into those problems translators have faced so far and their brilliant efforts of getting over the barriers together with their outcome in the literary world of Japan.

1. Some aspects of translation; in the case of Rabindranath

There is no doubt that works of Rabindranath Tagore have been translated the most into Japanese among Bengali poetry. The first translation of Rabindranth appeared in the magazine called *Zamboa* in February, 1913[1] and it should be noted that it was *before* Rabindranath received the Nobel Prize for literature. The translator was Mashino Saburo who indeed dedicated the rest of his life, which was no more than three years then though, to introduce this Bengali poet who was totally unknown to Japanese readers. Soon after the news that Rabindranth had received the Nobel Prize as the first non-European poet reached Japan, several other translations started to appear in various magazines in 1914. However, the real rush of publishing Rabindranath's poetry and other works was observed in 1915, caused by the expectation of Rabindranath's visit to Japan. The poet's visit was actually realized in the next year and these two years, 1915 and 1916, were the high peaks of such publications.

Here we can see an interesting phenomenon of acceptance of foreign literature. Only publishing a certain translation is, regardless of its quality, not enough for wide reception. It needs something more, a kind of special motive rooted in the background of its own culture. The first translation of Mashino and several others following after that did not raise any reaction, on the contrary, the whole literary world "remained silent" then.[2] Only a few months' later, the expectation of the visit of Rabindranath suddenly created a sensation and those works, which had been done before, started to be widely read. There also appeared other new translations at the time of this heated introduction of Rabindranath, however, there was no major gap of quality between the translations of the first stage and the new ones.

We also should not forget the fact that those were all second-hand translations from English. When Rabindranath translated his poetry himself, he dismissed the idea of presenting it in verse form and adopted the style of prose poem so that naturally those translations in Japanese were done in the same style. Most of the intellectuals *did* know that Rabindranath's original poetry was written in Bengali and some of them claimed that those second-hand translations were unable to reflect the poet's talent.

Although we can often find this kind of comment, that there should be a translation from the original text, no such translations came out until 1961[3] due to the simple fact that there was no single translator who could read the original Bengali. On the other hand, there appeared several versions of Japanese translations from Rabindranath's English poetry until then and one can safely assume that the one by Yamamuro Shizuka (1906-2000) was the most popular and widely read among them.

Yamamuro, who was a specialist of North European literature as well as a poet himself, became interested in Rabindranath's works in his youth and translated quite a lot of them and not only his poems, but also his short stories, essays and dramas. His first translation of Rabindranath's poetry came out in 1943, in the midst of the war period and 12 poems were expunged from the book by a strict censorship then. His second book was published in 1957, the third and the final book in 1966, which is still in the market. The second and the third book were based on each previous book though he continued to add new translations. In the end, the last book titled *Tagoru Shishu* (The Poetry of Tagore) contained 150 poems of his selection from *The Gardener, The Crescent Moon, Lover's Gift, Crossing, Stray Birds, Fireflies, Gitanjali, The Fugitive, A Flight of Swans, Fruit-Gathering, The Golden Boat* and *Selected Poems* published by Visva-Bharati.

Being a poet himself and having had quite a lot of experience of translation, Yamamuro's translation is fluent and his book has been widely read and still is quoted from time to time. Yamamuro's life long effort to introduce Rabindranath, especially those determined works during the war time, should not be undermined in the history of reception of Rabindranath. Still, the only drawback is, he could not read Bengali and all the translations were from English or French. This does not mean he totally ignored the importance of the original since he said: "There might be a question that all my translations are from English (only a few from

French) though the originals are written in Bengali. Even if those English poems were translated by the poet himself, the greater portion of the original taste might have been lost in these poems."[4]

However, at the same time he emphasizes the importance of English poems of Rabindranath and says:

> However, I am not saying this just because I cannot read Bengali, but those English poems might have become more clear and impressive than the original since the poet had to simplify the poetry. Through translation, the fluent expression of the original might have been lost, but there is a possibility that it strained the construction and essence of the poem. I dare say Indian poetry generally is too loquacious for us and we usually feel there are too many rhetorical phrases and so these simple English statements of his might be more familiar with Japanese readers. Moreover, they should be considered as English poetry by Rabindranath Tagore rather than usual translations from the original. Some people say those second-hand translations have little value, but I don't think it to be right.[5]

Only the readers who read both English and Bengali poetry of Rabindranath are capable of telling how and to what extent they are different from each other. True, Rabindranath knew well how to handle rhetorical phrases as well; but for instance, the original *Gitanjali* was written in as simple a style as possible with the extreme beauty of the structure and sound at the same time. It can hardly be said that English *Gitanjali* is more strained than the original *Gitanjali.*

The complexity is that, the English *Gitanjali* or other English poems, which are usually the texts of those translations, are also done by the same poet. No one can dismiss the value of these English versions and those are certainly more easily accessible to foreign readers. After all, this English version has its own significance as Buddhadeva Bose says: "*Gitanjali*'is a miracle of translation. The miracle is not that so much has survived; but the poems are re-born in the process, the flowers bloom anew on foreign soil."[6] Hence Yamamuro's indication that English poetry of Rabindranath is also his own creation is also right. What we must confirm here is, it only represents one side, which is rather minor, of the poet and the rest and major essence of the same poet's creation cannot be neglected in any case.

After the war, the second generation took the direct translation in hand along with the stream of re-appreciation of Rabidranath, and among them, Watanabe Shoko's[7] complete translation of *Gitanjali* is noteworthy since it was done from the original Bengali for the first time. This translation was first published in 1961 by Apolon-sha on the occasion of a hundred years of birth anniversary of the poet. The whole part was later issued in a paper-back series of Iwanami in 1977, which is one of the oldest and authorized series of world and Japanese literature. It was an epoch making publication and not only is it still available in the market, it is recognized as the most reliable book of Rabindranath's poetry.

The title of the book is, same as Yamamura's, *Tagoru shishu (The Poetry of Tagore)*. The striking feature of this book is that, Watanabe translated not only all the poems of original *Gitanjali*, but also translated once again all the poems of English *Gitanjali* as well, and presented both the translations in a single volume so that the readers can compare and recognize clearly the fundamental differences between the two. This presentation of his opened the eyes of readers regarding creative abilities of Rabindranath. He also added a detailed list of all the poems, that is, when and where each poem of the original *Gitanjali* was written, and also from which original Bengali text each English *Gitanjali* poem was translated.

Unlike Yamamuro, working with the original text, he emphasizes the difference between the original *Gitanjali* and the English *Gitanjali,* saying:

> If we pay attention to the style of poetry, we can easily notice that all 157 poems of the original *Gitanjali* were written in various fixed verse forms and had been meant for singing, whereas all 103 poems of English *Gitanjali* are prose poems. Out of 103, only 53 poems of the English *Gitanjali* were translated from original *Gitanjali'*and the rest were from his other Bengali poetry collections. In any case there are few pieces which can be called exact translations of the original Bengali. We see in this English text, many of the repetitions were omitted, peculiar words or phrases of Indian context were

replaced by English idiomatic phrases or style of saying, and sometimes even extra explanations were added.[8]

No one would deny that poetry should be appreciated in the original language and that even if one has to read it in translation, direct translation is much better than the secondhand one. The situation is a little complicated here, as we all know, since the English version of *Gitanjali* is also the work of the same poet. Like Yamamuro, Watanabe also says he considers English *Gitanjali* as an independent work of English literature.[9] The point is, the English *Gitanjali* and the original *Gitanjali* are completely different types of work by the same poet and that readers should know about it. In this context, Watanabe's above mentioned statement and the way of his presentation is quite helpful for understanding of Rabindranath better.

Commenting more on English *Gitanjali,* Watanabe says:

> On the whole, English *Gitanjali* was deliberately written for English readers. And this is because, even those 53 poems that are included in both the original and English give very different impressions. 14 more poems from the original *Gitanjali* were included in other English collections such as *The Gardener, Fruit Gathering and Lover's Gift and Crossing,* but still almost 90 poems of the original *Gitanjali* are not available in translation, which means the poet did not wish them to be read in English.
>
> The poems that were left out cannot be the ones the poet himself felt less confident about. We

rather can recognize the peculiarity or the greatness of the poet in these poems themselves. …… Those poems that had not been translated occupy a special position in his poetry and cannot be left out; even if those have been excluded from the English *Gitanjali*. Even those poems which carry almost the same meaning, they have become prose poems and expression itself has also become extremely simple in English. ……

This is the reason why I have placed the original Bengali *Gitanjali* as the main part of my translation here, and added the prose poems of English afterwards.[10]

Yamamuro guessed that "English statements of his might be more familiar with Japanese readers", but Watanabe, of course, had a different opinion. In this comment, he pointed out that the English *Gitanjali* was meant for English readers regarding not only the selection but also the expression. This may be a point which is rather overlooked, but should not be, when we do a second hand translation.

Here he implies that Japanese readers can appreciate those poems which were excluded from the English version and this kind of appreciation would lead them to a real understanding of Rabindranath's works. This was his belief and this belief forced him to complete this hard task of translating such a specific kind of poetry.

After all, these two translations of Watanabe's and Yamamuro's cannot be compared in the usual manner since these were done from respective texts which belonged to different kinds of creation. Still, we have to remember the fact that the English *Gitanjali* is a kind of work which tends to be cut off from the context of Bengali literature or historical background since these were meant for English readers as Watanabe pointed out. Of course, any poetic work is an individual product of the poet and there might be an idea that analysis of the text itself *is* the key to lead one to true realization and in that sense, there would be little necessity to know its cultural background to read those works deeply. But things are not so simple when one reads foreign poetry in translation. Especially in the case of Rabindranath, the English version of his poetry is often not a translation in a true sense so that this situation causes more misunderstandings and confusions.

It is quite likely that some adverse criticism toward Rabindranath in Japan could have been avoided if translations from the original were then published. For example, Kawahigashi Hekigoto, one of the leading Haiku poets of the time, once claimed that "we are disappointed for its lack of any acute cries of agony."[11] But he might have had a different impression if he had read whole works of original *Gitanjali* or other Bengali poems of Rabindranath. On the whole, readers of English works of Rabindranth have an impression of the poet as romantic, sentimental and somewhat otherworldly and many of the writers and poets in Japan actually dismissed Rabindranath's works being based on that image. On the other hand, some admirers of

Rabindranath *do* like the very image so that they tend to search for similar works which strengthen it and unconsciously dismiss other aspects that do not fit. It is quite difficult to sweep off the first image once it is evolved.

Incomplete knowledge about the cultural background also often results in unfortunate misunderstandings or confusions. Having known that many of Rabindranath's poems were meant for singing, Iwano Homei, a critic, once said; "Lyrics meant for singing cannot be poetry worth talking about."[12] Iwano was one of those critics who were extremely harsh to Rabindranath for some reason and we do not have to take this saying to the letter, however, it also cannot be denied that many readers were puzzled when they came to know that the original *Gitanjali* poems were actually songs. It is sometimes difficult to imagine that modern serious poetry *could* be a song especially in the culture where there is no similar style of literature.

Even Yamamuro, as we have seen already, did his work under a kind of incomplete knowledge though it did not affect him so much in a negative way. Not only did he say English *Gitanjali* "might have become more clear and impressive" than the original, he also dared to say that "Indian poetry generally is too loquacious for us."

It is not clear that on what basis he had this kind of impression, but we can at least say that Rabindranath's works are not always loquacious. Indeed, general readers in Japan are not fond of long and grand poems and rather prefer compact and dense expressions so that poets in Japan usually cut down their expressions to the very limit. Rabindranath himself found out this fact as we can see in his travelogue *Japan Yatri*.[13] Yet, this cannot be the reason that readers in Japan do not have to read Rabindranath's original poetry in Bengali.

If we turn our eyes to the difference in the taste, of course it creates another interesting phenomenon regarding the response of the readers. It is a well-known fact that Rabindranath often wrote short poems while in Japan and those works were published under the title of *Stray Birds* or *Lekhan*. They were hardly recognized as serious poetry back in Bengal, while they became quite popular in Japan or other countries. Rabindranath himself made some comments regarding *Lekhan* saying "Bengalis are used to read long and grand poems so that if the size of the poem is rather small, they cannot take it as a proper poem".[14] In the same writing, Rabindranath claims that some readers in Bengal used to count lines of *Gitanjali* or other poems and declared his miserliness in writing poems. The size of a certain poem seems a rather minor factor of the style of poetry, but at the same time it should not be totally ignored since it sometimes affects the reception of the work.

After all, we can hardly predict whether a certain translation will be well accepted or not since there are so many unstable factors. Not only in the case of Rabindranth, but also in other cases of renowned poets, there always remains a mystery when and why they are well accepted or not. A sincere work of translation is not always rewarded but on the other hand, there exists the so called apt translation which makes the work undying in a foreign language.

Unfortunately, Rabindranath has not had any translation of this level yet and it cannot be helped in a sense as there are only a small number of people who are involved in Bengali literature compared to others such as English, French or Russian literature. Still, even in those foreign literatures which have a longer history of translation, translators have found no simple answer for what is a good translation and how to work to create an apt translation.

The first translation of Bengali poetry, *Gitanjali* by Watanabe, appeared in 1961, while the first translation of English poetry came out in 1882 so that it won't be an irrelevant attempt if we look into a brief history of translation of poetry in Japan in order to have a view of future prospect of translating Rabindranath or any other Bengali poet. But before doing so, we should take a closer look into Watanabe's translation so as to make clear the barriers when one translates poetry into Japanese.

2. Translating poetry: Turning its rhythm into another

Gitanjali is a special poetry in many ways in Bengali literature. But its style, particularly that of "the perfect beauty" critics say[15], becomes the biggest barrier when someone tries to translate it. Watanabe was conscious about the verse form of original *Gitanjali* so that he had to devise some means to apply such a form into Japanese.

The trick he resorted to was the use of literary language in order to make a certain verse form in Japanese. He says:

> *Gitanjali* is meant for reciting and singing. I wanted to preserve the poetry form as much as possible, which meant keeping the number and the length of lines almost the same. I also wanted to make them fit for singing as they were in Bengali. Under this condition, I did not have any choice other than translating in literary form. I wonder what kind of Japanese language is appropriate for the poetry which is classical as well as familiar for ordinary people. My choice is only an attempt. Wishing someone in the future will translate these poems into colloquial verse with the cultivated style of the original, I will present this defective translation of mine.[16]

He was so conscious about the difference between English and original *Gitanjali* that he could never translate the original in prose style. This trial to present the closest style of the original led him to choose the literary form of the language.[17]

The problem is, the literary form of writing was completely abandoned in Japanese long before the publication of this book. In Japan, almost all the poems are written in the style of prose poem or colloquial free verse nowadays, except those traditional poems

162

such as Haiku. The fact that there is no specific metre in modern Japanese poetry makes it all the more difficult to translate any verses into Japanese. Of course, the translator knows the fact, so that he says this is an attempt. But it cannot also be denied that this style might keep some readers at a distance.

His vocabulary is generally plain but he could not help using some archaic words in the style of literary language. On the whole, his translation looks rather old fashioned even than the original though it has a certain fragrance of *Gitanjali*. Of course any translator will sympathize with him if he reads Watanabe's confession above, "did not have any choice other than translating in literary form" under the condition of trying to preserve the verse form of the original. What we should think now is if it is the only way to make a verse form and how to solve the problem of creating a certain rhythm in Japanese poetry in a colloquial form.

Not only in modern literature, Japanese poetry has long been rather pictorial than musical as Rabindranath keenly observed "all the poems I have heard so far are poems of seeing pictures, not of singing songs"[18] when he was in Japan in 1916. Even the traditional verse form like 'haiku' or 'waka' usually appears too short to preserve any specific metre and it may be hardly recognized as proper verse form for non-Japanese readers since there seems to be no repetition of a certain rhythm. This characteristic of Japanese poetry becomes the biggest barrier when one tries to translate foreign poetry and it can be said that Watanabe's attempt was

a kind of desperate resort to create some kind of a
rhythm in his translation. This barrier has always stood
in the way of translating foreign poetry, hence, it won't
be futile to trace some translations from European
languages here which have a longer history.

There is a famous translation theory by Futabatei
Shimei (1864-1909) who was an eminent writer and
also a translator of Russian literature. He was a pioneer
of translating western literature and his translation
greatly influenced the idea of literature or style of
writing in modern Japan. His short essay titled "My
standard of translation" has also influenced translators
in Japan a lot and is still quoted from time to time. The
most famous part of this writing is:

> I have never dismissed even one comma or period
> so that if there are three commas and one period in
> the original text, I made it a rule to use three commas
> and one period in my translation too. [19]

This part is usually quoted to show how much he was
attentive to preciseness, but that is rather too simplified
an interpretation and actually misses the point of his
idea. In the beginning of the same essay, Futabatei
indicates as follows:

> On the whole, western writings do not appeal
> so much when one only goes through them.
> However, if you once relish those writings you will
> find a kind of tone or melody and it will become
> clearer when you actually recite them that they are
> somewhat musical. That is why we can enjoy
> listening someone read aloud from western writings.

Actually, we can realize better what it means when we read silently, but even if we do not clearly understand the meaning of the sentence because of our lack of knowledge, we rather find it enjoyable to read aloud. This is certainly one feature of western writings. On the other hand, we do not have this kind of musical sense in our sentences...

Anyhow, once I decide to translate foreign writings, I think I must reflect the tone or rhythm of the original – this idea settled my standard style whenever I attempt to translate foreign writings...

When we try to translate any foreign works, if we only attend to its meaning and give too much weight to it, we could damage the rhythm of the original sentences. Therefore, I believed that I should first apprehend the rhythm of the original and then try to reflect it in my translation.[20]

The famous part which we have quoted before actually comes *after* this quotation, and it is clear what he emphasizes the most is how to reflect the original rhythm in his Japanese translation. Indeed he was not at all a believer of literal translation. At the end of the same essay, praising Zhukovsky's translation of Byron he recommends free translation rather irrespective of its original style if one can find out one's own rhythm.

Futabatei is not a specialist of translating poetry, he rather translated prose writings of great Russian writers but most of the renowned translators more or less have similar notions.

Japanese translation from foreign poetry, especially from western poetry is regarded to have started by

'Shintai shisho' (New Style Poetry) in 1882. This book consists of 14 translations of English poems by poets such as Shakespeare, Tennyson or Longfellow as well as 5 poems of the translator. This work was done with the rather enlightening purpose of encouraging new poetry in modern literature. Indeed, three translators[21] of this book were all professors of Tokyo Imperial University and none of them were scholars of literature. Therefore, translation itself was rather immature and they could use nothing but the traditional so called 7, 5 form [22] here.

Still, it has become a kind of stimulation of a new stream of poetry and many other serious translations of western poetry followed. Among them, three books are generally considered to be the most powerful and influential in the stream of modern Japanese poetry. These are, *Kaicho-on* (Sound of Sea Tide), *Sango-shu* (Collection of Corals) and *Gekka no ichigun* (A Throng Under Moon Light).

Kaicho-on, published in 1905, is definitely one of the first serious and genuine translation of western poetry. The translator was Ueda Bin (1874-1916), who was an English teacher of Tokyo Imperial University. Ueda was extremely good at foreign languages and fluent in English, French, German, Italian, Greek and Latin. *Kaicho-on* includes 57 poems from several European languages, and the poets he took up were 14 French, 7 German, 4 English, 3 Italian and one Provencal. Ueda apparently laid stress on French poetry and actually this was almost the first introduction of French poetry, especially to symbolist poetry. This translation greatly influenced modern Japanese poets, but interestingly, this book did not create an immediate sensation. Actually, the book was reprinted only once in 1908 and then after some years later gradually spread to general readers. In the end, this translation attained the fame of an apt translation after his death and has been read by generation after generation until the present time.

Ueda criticized the literary world of those days saying most of the literary men only pay attention to English Victorian poetry among European works. He also criticized the monotonous style of translation observed in 'Shintai shisho'. His translation was masterful, not only smooth but colorful at the same time using rather archaic words and very colloquial words. More than that, he created various meters which were not quite used in Japanese poetry.

As we can see from Ueda's saying "French poetry, by such as Verlaine, conveys a certain voice of music,"[23] he was sensitive about its musical elements. His translation always had a kind of meter which was not quite found in Japanese poetry before and with this rhythm, his translation stayed in people's mind for a long time. One of such translations was *Chanson d'Automne* by Verlaine and this one is still quoted often even at the present time. Not only he translated this poem in 3 stanzas with 6 lines each as it is in the original, but he applied simple 5, 5, 5, 5, 5, 5 meter as in the case of the first stanza "Akinohino Violonno

Tameikino Minishimite Hitaburuni Uraganashi". This style was fresh as well as easily recognized and it was granted that the translator conveyed its original rhythm successfully though it was not exactly the same.

The next masterwork of translation is *Sangoshu* by Nagai Kafu (1879-1959). Nagai, who became a renowned writer in later years, spent some years in America and France in his youth. After returning home, he published a kind of essays respectively named *Amerika Monogatari* (A Story of America, 1908) and *Furansu Monogatari* (A Story of France, 1909). Since then he started his writings seriously and a famous book of translation *Sangoshu* was published in 1913.

Though he was basically a prose writer, he was very much absorbed in French poetry when he was in France[24] and this passion for French poetry resulted in his translation. Nagai himself says; "I did those translations not because I wanted to import the fragrance of western poetry but because I thought it could be a help to polish my feelings and expressions."[25] The book contained 37 French poems of his favorite poets, and among them were works of Baudelaire, which was almost the first introduction to the literary world of Japan and which had a great response.[26]

Nagai's translation is elegant and highly appreciated though he does not so much attempt to apply various verse forms as Ueda did. At this stage, literary language was still in use for Japanese writings and Nagai also followed the custom. However, his language was nearer to colloquial language and sometimes he tried to write in the style of prose poems.

The opening poem of *Sangoshu* is the translation of *Le Mort joyeux* by Baudelaire, which is also the opening poem of his famous *Les Fleurs du mal*. The original poem is written in sonnet style but Nagai translated this poem rather freely. Translation also consists of 14 lines, however, there is no rhyme[27] and no rigid verse form. He uses rather longer units of phrase such as 10, 12, 13, 14 whereas 5 and 7 are the unit most used in Japanese as mentioned. This style actually fits in well with the specific poetic world of Baudelaire and anyhow, the spirit of this translation is believed to be succeeded to prominent poets such as Miki Rohu (1889-1964) or Hagiwara Sakutaro (1886-1942).

There is one more influential translation of poetry whose title is *Gekka no Ichigun*. The translator was Horiguchi Daigaku (1909-1981) and he again was a great lover of French poetry. Born as a son of a diplomat, Horiguchi spent many years in foreign countries including France. Moreover, his step-mother was a Belgian lady and French was the language spoken in his family. Thus he had no difficulty in reading French literature whereas he had to struggle to find out the proper literary style of Japanese. Fortunately his father was a highly cultivated person and had quite a wide range of collection of books. Living abroad most of his youth, he acquired high cultivation of Japanese literature.

He started translating poetry in his very youth while he was abroad for his own pleasure and later published quite a lot of translations. He also wrote his own poetry[28] and essays, but is now rather well known as a translator not because he was a minor poet but because he was such a distinguished translator.

His most famous translation, *Gekka no Ichigun* was published in 1925 and Horiguchi presented 340 poems of 66 French poets in the book. It looks almost like the anthology of modern French poetry though the selection depends completely upon his taste. The book contains not only the works of those poets who were already introduced such as Baudelaire, Verlaine, Valery, but also many other poets who were unknown to Japanese readers then such as Apollinaire, Cocteau and Radiguet. Horiguchi shows true genuine of translation in these poems of modernism, especially in Apollinaire and Cocteau's poetry. Indeed, this modernist poetry in translation has become a wellspring of the stream of modernism in Japanese poetry.

There are many popular poems in this book which are still quoted at the present time and Le Pont Mirabeau by Apollinaire is certainly one of those poems which have been loved by many readers. Horiguchi once called Apollinaire's poetry as 'musical lyric' and naturally his translation also has supreme rhythm of his own though he did not apply any specific verse form. Language itself has become almost natural colloquial Japanese here. His literary style, simple as well as elegant getting into a natural rhythm, has become a kind of milestone of translation and even the translators today consider it as a model.

Observing these processes of translations, it must be admitted that Watanabe's translation in literary language is untimely and old-fashioned. It is rather queer that he did not apply natural colloquial language long after the great success of *Gekka no Ichigun* even if it is the first attempt to translate any poem from the Bengali language. He was a scholar of Buddhism and Indian Philosophy, yet, he should have read those translations from French poetry as an intellectual of the time. Of course Rabindranath's poetry itself has a different ambience from that of the works of modernism and that can be one of the reasons that Watanabe adopted a completely different style. Still, it is also true that there is an expectation for further trial of translation as Watanabe himself admitted.

As mentioned before, Horiguchi's translation of Le Pont Mirabeau by Apollinaire is widely admitted as one of the apt translations. Still, this poem was translated again and again even after that and we can read more than 10 versions of the same poem. Rabindranath's *Gitanjali* is also such a masterpiece worth translating over and over again and we should at least have scope for further attempts.

Conclusion:

We have so far roughly surveyed both the Japanese translations of Rabindranath's poetry and of some western poetry. Needless to say, there are many aspects and factors in translating poetry such as symbols, metaphors etc. whereas I could only refer to the rhythm of Japanese translation. We have to yield to other aspects of translation to another piece of writing; however, the rhythm is definitely a major fact in translating in the case of poetry.

It has always been said that translating poetry is almost impossible while many of them have been actually translated. Trial and error of those translations are the bridge between the impossible and the possible and all the translations including those that look unsuccessful are indeed valuable attempts to discover a new horizon of literature. As Japanese readers discovered Baudelaire by Nagai's translation or discovered Apollinaire by Horiguchi's translation, they have discovered Rabindranath by Yamamuro's or Watanabe's translation. And there always will be a new discovery when it is translated afresh, therefore, there will be no limit of new trials.

Notes:

1) Mashino Saburo (1889-1916, poet and translator), 'Indo koshi' (Old poems of India), *Zanboa*, 3, no.2 (February, 1913): 45-52. There might have been a kind of confusion about the author at this point. Mashino titled his translation 'Old poems of India' here, but at the same time he clearly mentioned the name of the poet as 'Rabindranath Tagore of Bengal'.

2) Uchigasaki Sakusaburo (1877-1947, critic and a translator of some of the works of Rabindranath), 'Tagoru to Indo-bunka'

(Tagore and Indian Culture), *Rikugo Zasshi*, 35, no.5 (May, 1915): 2-9. In this article, Uchigasaki himself recollected the literary world of Japan "remained silent and there was no reaction or comment."

3) The translation from the original *Gitanjali* was done by Watanabe Shoko in 1961 and this was the first attempt to translate Bengali poetry. We are going to discuss about this translation later. As for prose writing, Sano Jinnosuke translated *Gora* from the original and published it much earlier in 1929.

4) Yamamuro Shizuka, *Tagoru Shishu* (Tokyo: Yayoi Shobo, 1966), 175.

5) ibid., 176.

6) Buddhadeva Bose, *Kabi Rabindranath* (Kolkata: Dey's Publishing, 1970), 89.

7) Watanabe Shoko (1907-77) was a famous scholar of Buddhism and knowing Sanskrit and other foreign languages, learned Bengali almost himself as well.

8) Watanabe Shoko, *Tagoru shishu* (Tokyo : Iwanami shoten, 1977), 3.

9) ibid., 388.

10) ibid., 4-5.

11) Kawahigashi Hekigoto, 'Tagoru no insho' (The Impression of Tagore), *Nihon oyobi nihonjin* 683 (July, 1916): 135.

12) Iwano Homei, 'Tagoru-shi ni chokugen su' (An Appeal to Tagore), *Yomiuri shinbun*, 16-7, June, 1916.

13) In his travelogue *Japan Yatri*, Rabindranath talks about its nature to "condense one's expressions (nijer prakashke atyanta sankhipt karte thaka)" quoting Matsuo Basho's Haiku. Rabindranath Tagore, *Japan Yatri* (Kolkata: Visva-Bharati, 1974), 82-3.

14) Rabindranath Tagore, Lekhan, *Rabindra Racanabali vol 14* (Kolkata: Visva-Bharati, 1942), 528.

15) For example, Buddhadeb Bose says "When we observe perfect work like 'Gitanjali', we don't feel like adding anything there." Buddhadeb Bose, *Kabi Rabindranath,* 74.

16) Watanabe Shoko, *Tagoru shishu,* 387.

17) Actually, Watanabe did not follow any kind of fixed verse form in his translation. For example, the form in the first stanza of 67th poem of *Gitanjali* is: 5,5 / 5,7 / 3,6 / 2,6 / 2,7 / 3,7. He sometimes uses 5 and 7 feet which are regular in the Japanese tradition, but avoided it consisting only 5 and 7 which would be monotonous for modern readers.

18) Rabindranath Tagore, *Japan Yatri*, 82. Rabindranath, of course, indicates its pictorial feature of poetic expression, but here we should point out another pictorial factor in *writing* poetry in Japanese language. This factor lies in the writing system of using different kind of characters which is rather complicated. In Japanese, three kinds of characters, respectively named 'hiragana', 'katakana' and 'kanji', are used altogether. 'kanji' is Chinese character which is ideographical and both 'hiragana' and 'katakana' are Japanese character which is phonetic. The trick is, a certain word can be written in each of these three characters so that there is a choice how we write a certain word. In prose writing, there is somewhat a standard of choosing characters, but in poetry, it is almost free to write in any character. For example, 'mizu', a word for water, *can be* written in any of these three characters and if it is written in 'hiragana' it *looks* soft whereas in 'kanji' it *looks* rather stiff. This word is not usually written in 'katakana' since 'katakana' is a character for foreign words, however, if the poet dares to use 'katakana' for 'mizu', and actually sometimes does, it can give queer or distinct impression to readers. On the whole, the choice of characters can create very much different impression and poets are usually concerned about it. Moreover, this word 'mizu' is written in two letters in 'katakana' or 'hiragana' while in 'kanji' in one letter. It means that the shorter the sentence will appear the more 'Kanji' one uses though phonetically these two sentences

are exactly the same. This is only a part of the technique in *writing* poetry and anyway, poets in Japanese have to be very keen about how it *looks* as well as how it *sounds*. This technique of writing a certain sentence is naturally applied by translators also.

19) Futabatei Shimei, 'Yo ga honyaku no hyojun' (My standard of translation), *Futabatei Shimei zenshu 5* (Tokyo: Iwanami Shoten, 1966), 174.

20) ibid., 173-4.

21) One of these three translators was Inoue Tetsujiro (1856-1944), a scholar of philosophy, who later criticized a lot about Rabindranath especially his view on civilization.

22) Traditional Japanese verse form almost always consists of 7 and 5 feet as in the case of 'haiku'. 'Haiku' consists of only 5, 7, 5 and a longer form called 'tanka' is written in 5, 7, 5, 7, 7. There was even longer form in the past, but 7 and 5 have always been the unit of the verse form in Japan.

23) Ueda Bin, *Kaicho-on* (Tokyo: Tokyo-do, 1905), 76.

24) During the period of his stay in France (1907-8), he came to know Ueda Bin.

25) Nagai Kafu, 'Yakushini tsuite' (about my translation) in Kamei and Kutsukake ed. *Meishi Meiyaku Monogatari* (Tokyo: Iwanami Shoten, 2005), 87.

26) At the time of Rabindranath's visit to Japan for the first time in 1916, Iwano, a critic, mentioned before, criticized Rabindranat's works saying those cannot have any impact in Japan whose literary men were already familiar with symbolism of French poetry (Iwano Homei, 'Tagoru-shi ni chokugen su' (An Appeal to Tagore). He did not mention any name of the poet here, but naturally, he should have made this remark bearing the translation such as *Sangosho* or *Kaicho-on* in his mind.

27) Structure of Japanese language is not fit for rhyme and there has never been any attempt to rhyme in verse in Japanese anyway.

28) Along with the translation he always wrote his own poems and his first book of poetry, *Gekko to Piero* (Moonlight and a clown, 1919) was also highly appreciated.

Bibliography

- Buddhadeb Bose, *Kabi Rabindranath*, Kolkata, Dey's Publishing, 1970.

Works cited:

- Futabatei Shimei, 'Yo ga honyaku no hyojun' (My standard of translation), *Futabatei Shimei zenshu 5*, Tokyo, Iwanami Shoten, 1966.

- Hara Takuya & Nishinaga Yoshinari ed., *Honyaku Hyakunen (A Hundred Years of Translation)*, Tokyo, Taishukan Shoten, 2000.

- Iwano Homei, 'Tagoru-shi ni chokugen su (An Appeal to Tagore)', *Yomiuri shinbun*, 16-7, June, 1916.

- Kamei Shunsuke & Kutsukake Yoshihiko ed., *Meishi Meiyaku Monogatari* (Story About Excellent Poems and Apt Translation), Tokyo, Iwanami Shoten, 2005.

- Kawahigashi Hekigoto, 'Tagoru no insho' (The Impression of Tagore), *Nihon oyobi nihonjin* 683 (July, 1916):135.

- Horiguchi Daigaku tr., *Gekka no Ichigun* (A Throng Under Moonlight), Tokyo, Kodansha, 1996.

- Mashino Saburo tr., 'Indo koshi' (Old poems of India), *Zanboa*, 3, no.2 (February, 1913): 45-52.

- Mashino Saburo tr., *Indo shinshishu Gitanjali* (New Poetry of India, Gitanjali), Tokyo, Toundo shoten, 1915.

- Nagai Kafu tr., *Sango-shu* (Collection of Corals), Tokyo, Iwanami Shoten, 1991.

- Rabindranath Tagore, *Japan Yatri*, Kolkata, Visva-Bharati, 1974.

- Rabindranath Tagore, Lekhan, *Rabindra Racanabali 14*, Kolkata, Visva Bharati, 1942.

- Ueda Bin tr., *Kaicho-on* (Sound of Sea Tide), Tokyo: Tokyo-do, 1905.

- Watanabe Shoko tr., *Tagoru Shishu* (Poetry of Tagore), Tokyo, Iwanami Shoten, 1977.

- Yamamuro Shizuka tr., *Tagoru Shishu* (Poetry of Tagore), Tokyo, Yayoi Shobo, 1966.

- Yoshida Seiichi ed., *Meiji Taisho Yakushishu* (Translation of Poetry in Meiji and Taisho era), Tokyo, Kadokawa Shoten, 1971.

Chronological Record

- 1882 *Shintai Shishu* published
- 1905 *Kaicho-on* published
- 1913 *Sango-shu* published
- 1913 first translation of Rabindranath's poem printed
- 1914 first translation of English *Gitanjali* published
- 1916 Rabindranath's first visit to Japan

- 1924 Rabindranath's second visit to Japan
- 1925 *Gekka no Ichigun* published
- 1929 Rabindranath's third visit to Japan
- 1943 Yamamuro's translation of English poetry of Rabindranath published
- 1961 first translation of original *Gitanjali* by Watanabe published